The Irish Words You Should Know

Hector Ó hEochagáin is a TV and radio presenter. He has been travelling the world for TG4 for 23 years and co-hosted one of Ireland's most popular podcasts, *The Tommy, Hector & Laurita Podcast*. He lives in Galway.

The Irish Words You Should Know*

HECTOR Ó hEOCHAGÁIN

*And how to use them every day

GILL BOOKS

Gill Books
Hume Avenue
Park West
Dublin 12
www.gillbooks.ie

Gill Books is an imprint of M.H. Gill and Co.

© Hector Ó hEochagáin 2024

978 07171 99860

Designed by www.grahamthew.com
Edited by Catherine Gough
Copy edited by Esther Ní Dhonnacha
Proofread by Dorothy Ní Uigín and Bríd Nowlan
Printed and bound in Great Britain by Clays Ltd, Elcograf S.p.A.
This book is typeset in Freight Text Pro by Typo•glyphix

The paper used in this book comes from the wood pulp of sustainably managed forests.

All rights reserved.
No part of this publication may be copied, reproduced or transmitted in any form or by any means, without written permission of the publishers.

To the best of our knowledge, this book complies in full with the requirements of the General Product Safety Regulation (GPSR). For further information and help with any safety queries, please contact us at productsafety@gill.ie.

A CIP catalogue record for this book is available from the British Library.

Do mo mhamaí Trina,
mo dhaidí Michael agus mo dheartháir Freddy.

Author's note

The Irish in the book is the Irish that I speak, which is Connemara Irish by way of Ráth Chairn. It's spoken, colloquial Irish and, since some of the words and phrases don't even appear in dictionaries, it wasn't always possible to confirm spellings. The phrases in this book are intended for spoken use, and the pronunciation is of the Connemara variety.

Contents

Introduction: Claim your inheritance, feed your imagination   9

1. The many ways to say hello in Irish   13
2. Words to take you on an adventure   55
3. Emotional words for every mood   95
4. Words from Gaeltacht days   139
5. On Inis Meáin time   175
6. Words for romancing   211
7. Words for the back of your knee and other body parts   241
8. Upgrade your Irish insults   271
9. Words for Ireland's uniquely unreliable weather   305
10. The *cúpla focal* for going about your day   345
11. Lucky dip   383

Afterword: Irish is a superpower – use it every day   414

Introduction: Claim your inheritance, feed your imagination

Language has been with us from the beginning of time. It's like a massive global warehouse of culture and knowledge, our passport to delve deeper into new worlds. Communication is a vital part of being human, and language connects us, breaks down barriers, and shows who we are. I've always tried my best to learn a small bit of the local language on my journeys around the world while filming the TV show on TG4. To be able to shake hands, smile, and chat in the local language means a lot to me, and it shows the stranger standing in front of me who I am. It's me being human. Language is more powerful than any computer program, and in this world of smartphone domination and artificial intelligence, it's never been as important to use and preserve our languages.

    The Irish language is our inheritance. It lives underneath us in the soil, it blows through the leaves on trees and rises from the roots, it's in the wind and the rain, in the water and the waves, it's in our stone and our mountains, our sun and our sky. Irish was part of this island before English, it's the language of our tribes, and it tells us about our ancestors and our land. It explains to us in so many ways who we are.

Many of the words I've included in this book are a product of the environment, especially the sea. Irish is the great recycler – we have taken words for nature and repurposed them to describe how we feel. *'Loinnir'*, a word that describes the sunlight sparkling on the waves, is used to capture that merriness you feel after early pints of stout in the morning. Irish people are great storytellers, whether it's in our literature or down the pub, and you can see that love of storytelling embedded in our national language. So many Irish phrases are like tiny poems; they tell whole stories in a few words. Even if you're not an Irish-speaker, the way Irish people speak English has been influenced by the Irish language and has made us masters of conversation. And that's what this book is all about – conversation.

I was no swot in school. I got a C in Irish in the Leaving Cert and failed first year of Early and Modern Irish in Trinity College Dublin. I was never great at writing Irish, but by God could I speak it. My ability with the language came from being put in the right location. People think I grew up in an Irish-speaking household, but none of my family were Irish-speakers, bar the odd word here and there. I was sent off to the Gaeltacht at eight years old, and that's where the seed was planted. And it grew and grew until Irish eventually landed me a job travelling the world for a brand-new TV station. But I'm still a student of the language, always will be, and some of the words I've included are new to me too. I've learned them from trying to find new ways to describe the places I travel to and the people I meet there, so that viewers at home in their living rooms can hear what the Amazon or Papua New Guinea is like through Irish. And I've realised that if there are many ways to say something in English, there are hundreds of ways to say it in Irish.

When I say the words and phrases in this book, they conjure up images in my head that feed my imagination. Even the rain feels wetter *as Gaeilge*. There has to be some part of our brain that reacts to language and paints a picture when we hear it. That's how I've chosen the phrases you're about to read – I want to paint a picture in your head through Irish. But sometimes I've included phrases just because I'm in love with how they sound. They're timeless words for the long adventure of life. I want you to use them in your house, in your classroom, and in your parish. And then spread them to the next generation.

Most of all, I don't want you to be afraid to use them. I'm not judgemental about how much Irish you have – how could I be after failing out of college? It doesn't matter to me what level you are, whether you're opening up Duolingo to learn the basics or you've decided to go back to learn Irish at the age of 47, whether you're studying it in college or teaching it in school. This book is for everyone. You might use these phrases to make your spoken Irish more fluent, or you could just drop a word or two into your conversations in English to make them more playful and fun. I want you to enjoy using Irish, and I know that when you read about the words you'll see the magic in the language that I do. And if you happen to see me out and about in the shops or at the airport, please come up to me and say one of the phrases from this book. It could be *'lig do scíth'* (take a rest) or *'sceallóga'* (chips) – it doesn't matter. Knowing you picked it up here would make my day.

There's no language in the world that can be translated directly into English, and this is definitely the case with Irish. I've searched for ways in English to do justice to these Irish phrases, and so I've done my best to show you through stories how you might use them in your daily life. I've included a phonetic version of them, too, so that you have a good idea of how to pronounce them. In Connacht and Ulster, fluent speakers often pronounce *'agat'* as 'att' instead of 'ah-gut' and *'agam'* as 'awm' instead of 'ah-gum' so, if you're from those areas, that's one way to level up your fluency. But don't worry too much about getting the sounds right, and please don't be embarrassed to give it a go. Even just reading about the words, whether you use them or not, will give you a new perspective on the land, the weather, relationships, feelings, and even the body. I can't wait for your mind to start creating images as you read about the words, and I want you to dive into those images, to really understand the power of the words as they make their way from the page to your brain. They could be as basic as *'scaití'* (the odd time) or as profound as *'in ísle brí'* (at a low ebb); either way there's a beauty in them.

Think of this book as a spice rack and you want to make a curry, but you have no turmeric or cumin or paprika. I'm giving you all the spices you need to make a good curry, so the way you use Irish will have flavour and depth.

I'm so excited that I can give you this, because the Irish language has been my friend for a long time. It has nurtured me and cared for me, made me laugh and made me cry, it's lifted me and guided me, pushed me and advised me. It's a friend that's opened doors for me, educated me, and brought me on adventures. It's moulded me, strengthened me, and taught me about life. It's always been there for me, sitting beside me in the car and on planes. It's funny, it's dark, it's sarcastic, it's deep, it's smart, it's wild, it's giddy, it's soft, it's powerful, it's dramatic, it's subtle and it's soulful. Irish is colourful, layered, mystical and enlightening. Irish has been with me since I was a young lad, like my own private Gaeltacht in my heart and in my head. It has opened my eyes and filled my mind, and now I want to fill your mind too.

ONE

The many ways to say hello in Irish

How many different ways do we greet each other in English? We rarely say 'hello' or 'goodbye'; it's much more casual than that. How's it going? Story? What's the craic? Good luck. Talk to ya. There's no problem with saying *'dia duit'*, but there are a million other ways to say 'hello' in Irish, and the best of them come from Connemara. Imagine yourself at a checkpoint in the Gaeltacht and instead of guards checking your NCT and tax there are language police waiting to see how you greet them. And I guarantee you, if you lean out the car window and say, *'Cén chaoi a bhfuil tú?'*, they'll not only wave you through, they'll probably tell you what the big news in the parish is as well. It's like getting a visa in your passport for the Republic of Connemara.

The phrases in this chapter will take you from a chipper in An Spidéal to the boat to the Aran Islands, and you can throw out a *'tóg go réidh é'* (take it handy) on Reek Sunday when you're passing the other climbers on Croagh Patrick. When you translate many of these Irish phrases into English, they boil down to wishing good luck and health to someone in the most creative ways.

This is a whole new world of hellos and goodbyes, and you'll be King of the *Sláinte*s in the pub as well.

Aon scéal agat/'ad?
Any stories?

[ayn shcale ah-gut *or* ayn shcale att]

Aon scéal agat?
Diabhal scéal muna bhfuil scéal 'ad fhéin.
Any stories?
I've no story unless you've a story for me yourself.

The greeting you say to someone you know well.

If *'cád é an scéal?'* is primary-school Irish, *'aon scéal agat'* is college level. It means, 'Any stories, any craic?', and you have to pronounce *'agat'* as 'att' to make it sound right. It has that Connemara sharpness, where people speak a hundred miles a minute. It's the greeting you say to someone you know well. You bump into a friend outside the local shop and give each other one of those little shoulder hugs men do: 'What's the craic?' It's an ice-breaker of a hello.

This is one of those call-and-response greetings too, though the response is such deep Connemara Irish that you would rarely hear it. *'Diabhal scéal muna bhfuil scéal 'ad fhéin?'* I've the devil's story unless you have one for me yourself. I don't know why the devil comes into it, but it's like saying, 'Nothing much unless you have one yourself'. It reminds me of how in the midlands, when you have next to none of something, you say, 'Divil a bit.' 'Got any cash on ya, Hector?' 'Divil a bit.' Not a shred.

Cén chaoi a bhfuil tú?
In what way are you?

[cane qwee a will too ***or*** cyan ee will too]

Cén chaoi a bhfuil tú, Hector?
Níl caill ar bith orm.
How are you, Hector?
I'm grand, not a bother on me.

A phrase is for when you see the postman stopping by on a cold winter's morning.

There's so much rhythm to this phrase, and it sounds best when it rolls off the tongue and you only pronounce half of it, like a true local. If you pronounce it 'cain qwee a will too', there's no doubt you're learning Irish from Duolingo. It has to be 'cyan ee will too', proper distilled Connemara pronunciation. The pitch evokes the mountains and rivers of the west. If you say it this way, I can tell almost straight away what part of the country you're from.

This phrase is for when you see the postman stopping by on a cold winter's morning, or the *Bean an Tí* welcoming the kids back from the day at the local *halla*. You can imagine sitting by your *currach*, sipping the last of the *poitín*, the evening closing in, and you bump into your neighbour. It's 'cyan ee will too' or nothing else.

There are a few handy answers you can keep up your sleeve if you're ever asked *'Cén chaoi a bhfuil tú?'* They are all throw-the-head back, eyes-to-Heaven answers. You hardly need to say most of them, but they're best accompanied with an upward nod of the head and a sharp intake of breath.

Dia linn, Dia linn is Muire, Dia linn is Muire is capall bán fút
God bless you, God and Mary bless you, God and Mary bless you and may you have a white horse underneath you

[dee-a linn, dee-a linn iss mwih-ra, dee-a linn iss mwih-ra iss cop-al bawn fu-at]

Achoo!
Dia linn.
Achoo!
Dia linn is Muire.
Achoo!
Dia linn is Muire is capall bán fút.

Achoo!
God bless you.
Achoo!
God and Mary bless you.
Achooooo!
God and Mary bless you and may you have a white horse underneath you.

For the serial sneezer in the group.

Maybe you're sitting in the pub and someone in your company sneezes. And you don't give it much thought. *'Dia linn.'* But then that same person comes back with a second sneeze, and the alarm bells go off. The second sneeze can often be the giveaway ... The assailant sneezes a third time so you know what you're dealing with here is a very serious situation. A serial sneezer. I've travelled the world with my producer Evan Chamberlain, who's a serial sneezer. He regularly hits 10 or 12 – I know this because me and Rosco count. It's one of the most embarrassing things when he gets going and you're somewhere like the office of the head of a NASA space station in French Guiana.

I learned this phrase in the Gaeltacht when I was 12 and it's come in handy, because there's a serial sneezer in every group. Once is fine, twice you can excuse, but three or more times in a row and you're walking away pretending you don't know them. You could even add to this depending on how extreme the sneezing is. The whole cast of characters from the Bible could be there: 'God be with you and Mary and Joseph and the three wise men and the baby Jesus'. But you always have to finish with the white horse so they can ride away out of the pub because they're making a holy show of themselves.

Caidé mar atá tú?
What about you?

[ka-jay mar a-taw too]

Bhuel a mhac, caidé mar atá tú?
Maith go leor, caidé mar atá tú féin?
Well, how're things?
Grand, how're things with you?

As Kneecap would say it up North.

This is a shout-out to all my Irish-speaking brothers and sisters up in the North. You'll need to put away your *'conas atás'* and take this one out of your locker if you're in Northern Ireland. It's pronounced as 'J mar ataw too' *i mBéal Feirste* – you barely even say the first 'c'. There's been a swell of Gaeilge in the North, thanks to the massive effort put in over the years by teachers and Gaeilgeoirs to have the language recognised. There's a great feeling of culture and language identity, and it's from young people coming up through the education system learning Irish. The *Féile an Phobail* in August every year is fantastic for celebrating the language, with almost 20,000 people, from all backgrounds, coming together for the week-long festival.

The Belfast Gaeltacht is thriving, and you can't mention Irish in Belfast without talking about the band Kneecap. They've been doing their thing, rapping in the Irish language over the last few years, and now they're touring the world, spreading that lovely, powerful Northern Irish dialect.

Go dtarrthaí Dia sinn
God save us

[gu dawrr-hee dee-a shin]

Go dtarrthaí Dia sinn! Breathnaigh ar an leaid seo, tá sé caochta.
God save us and bless us! Will ya look at the state of yer man, he's drunk as a skunk.

A greeting for the kind of people who have a picture of Pope John Paul II with the flickering yellow light underneath him.

This one is for the Irish women of a certain vintage who have a great relationship with the Lord. And when they roll it out, you know something bad has happened.

My mother, Tríona, was happiest when she was praying. She had Bibles placed in strategic locations all around the house, always to have easy access. She used to write little cards with her own interpretations of excerpts of the Bible on them, like she was trying to decipher what was being said and put it in plain language. When she died and we'd go back to the house, we'd keep finding these cards, like she'd left them there for us. She was a woman of faith who was still partial to a profanity, and she would have loved this phrase. It's for the people who might have a picture of Pope John Paul II with that flickering yellow light underneath it, but they still lash out a 'JESUS CHRIST ALMIGHTY' if something bad happens. It's a perfect one for when the washing blows off the line and gets ruined.

Go dtarrthaí Dia sinn. God save us!

Dia dhá réiteach!
Holy God!/Oh Lord!

[dee-a gaw raytach]

Dia dhá réiteach, ná déan sin! Scanraigh tú an t-anam asam.
Holy God, don't do that, you scared the soul clean out of me.

When you open the door to the toilet in the pub and bump into someone already on their way out.

This is a phrase used to express shock, in the little moments when you open the door to the toilet in the pub and bump into someone already on their way out, or when a child jumps out from behind a bush and scares the living daylights out of you. But it can be used for the epic surprises as well. Like when the son or daughter flies home from Australia for Christmas, arrives in Dublin Airport in secret, drives four hours to the family home, sneaks in through the patio door, and you're standing there making the brandy sauce without a clue as to what's going on. You turn around and there they are ... *'Dia dhá réiteach!'*

Tóg go réidh é
Take her handy

[towg go ray ay]

Tóg go réidh é, feichfidh mé Dé hAoine thú.
Take it easy, see you on Friday.

One of my favourite ways of saying goodbye.

I use *'Tóg go réidh é'* all the time when I'm leaving somewhere. It's one of my favourite ways of saying goodbye. It's just a lovely, casual way of going, 'Right, man. Talk to you. Take it easy. Take it handy.' It's like *'hasta luego'* in Spanish. You walk away a few yards and shout it back over your shoulder.

It's great for when your friend has stayed with you for the weekend and you've had an unbelievable catch up. It's full of familiarity. You're saying goodbye with the knowledge that you're going to see them again soon. You can inject it with a bit of a warning as well, though, when your son or daughter is pulling away in the car to do their driving test and you have a last little knock on the window. *'Tóg go réidh é.'* Take her handy.

Slán go fóillín
All the best

[slawn guh fo-leen]

Sin é mar sin, beidh mé ag caint leat. Slán go fóillín, darling.
That's it then, be chatting to ya. See ya soon, darling.

A great big hug of a farewell.

This is pretty much like saying, 'See you in a while-een' in English. It's Claddagh talk that's spilled over into general Galway Irish.

If you put '*-ín*' at the end of anything in Irish, it adds a bit of affection to the phrase, like 'Come here to me, loveen' or calling someone '*mo stóirín*', which means 'my little darling'. In Galway, the River Corrib divides the city, and anything at the far side of the river is known as 'Back the Wesht'. Once you cross over the bridge at Spanish Arch, you're heading for Connemara. Phrases like this started in Connemara and would have worked their way back into Galway City over the centuries, so you hear them around a lot. The beauty of adding '-ín' to something is that you can use it in English *or* Irish.

'*Slán go fóillín*' is very much a short goodbye, full of love, that's said with a warm embrace. A great big hug of a farewell.

Beidh muid ag caint/ beidh mé ag caint leat
I'll be talking to you

[by mwij egg kaynt]

Beidh mé abhaile arís ag deireadh na míosa. Sea, an Aoine. Slán a ghrá, beidh mé ag caint leat, slán slán slán slán ...
I'll be home at the end of the month so. Yeah, the Friday. Love ya, be talkin' to ya, bye bye bye bye ...

*A lovely way to end
a phone conversation.*

This is the beautiful moment when the big day has arrived for the winter: your local oil man who you've known for years is here. He's filled up the tank, hopped back in the truck, and he's heading away. And you go, 'Cheers. I'll be talking to you.' It's saying, 'I'll be here in a few months' time when you're back to top up the oil again.' It's also a lovely way to end a phone conversation, or when you're delighted with a job someone has done in the house. You've finally got a plumber to fix that leaky pipe and you're happy because you got that little task done, so you say, *'Beidh muid ag caint,'* when you're seeing them off. 'I'll be talking to ya.'

Fágfaidh muid mar sin é
Sure we'll leave it there/I think we're done here

[faw-guh mwij mar shin ay]

Ceart go leor mar sin, a leaids, fágfaidh muid mar sin é.
Beimid ag traenáil arís ag a 7.30 ar an Luan.
Right, lads , we will leave it there. We train again Monday night at 7.30.

When it's four o'clock on a Friday and you need to get out of that meeting before someone else starts talking.

This is a shout-out to the Microsoft Teams posse, the Zoom posse, and the Google Meets posse, who have gone out of their fucking minds because they spent the last four years on video conferences looking at people on laptops all over the country. You've had a three-hour meeting that's gone round and round in wishy-washy waffle, Barry still can't get his mic off mute, and you've had an intimate view of Mary's nostrils for the afternoon. It's four o'clock on a Friday and you've lost the will to live, then someone says 'Right ...' and you know that's it. The end. You need to get out of that meeting before someone else starts talking. 'Sure look, it's best we wrap up here, lads. We'll leave it there.' *'Fágfaidh muid mar sin é'* is a conversation closer, there's no doubt about it.

Fada an lá
Long time no see

[fa-da on law]

Fada an lá ó chonaic mé thú!
Haven't seen ya in years!

There's no need for any other language around it.

You can walk up to someone, shake their hand, and deliver this phrase without saying anything else at all. It's used up and down the country every day of the week. You walk into the pub on Christmas Eve and see your school friend, or you run into an old colleague in a hotel lobby. 'Jaaaaysus, would you look who it is. I haven't seen you in years.' *Fada an lá*. There's no need for any other language around it. It's a great way to say hello that has plenty of information packed into it: it's a lovely surprise to bump into you after all this time.

Bhuel?
Well?

[well]

Bhuel ? Aon chraic?
Well? Any craic?

A question that doesn't expect an answer.

This one hardly needs a translation. In all its shortness, there's an intimacy to this phrase. You know the person well or you see them regularly if you greet them with '*Bhuel?*' It's a question that doesn't expect an answer.

I use 'Well?' with Tommy Tiernan in 99 per cent of my texts. I could be filming in the Philippines and he could be doing a gig in New York and I text him 'Well' and he will come back with 'Well'. We wouldn't say anything else, but that's enough for me because I can hear the accent coming out 100 per cent. We said 'Well' when we met in first year, and we said 'Well' throughout the rest of secondary school. We would say it to each other all the time in Navan. That's the way we say hello. When I hear somebody going, 'Well, Hector,' that's pure Dean Cogan or O'Growney Terrace or St Brigid's, all the real old parts of Navan town. I can practically hear people talking in their Navanese. '*Bhuel*' is used as much in Irish as it is in English, so it will take you anywhere.

Maith go leor
That'll do

[mah gu lyor]

Tá mé théis an tanc a líonadh ansin, beidh tú go breá anois don gheimhreadh.
Maith go leor.
So I've filled up the tank there, now you're good at least for the winter.
That'll do.

A *universal farewell*.

This is the equivalent of saying, 'That's grand, no bother' in English. You can say it after knocking on a door to leave in a parcel and you find you're at the wrong house. 'Is this the Cunninghams'?' 'No, no, they're next door.' It's a handy one for the DPD drivers. Someone might call to your door to sell you broadband, but you already have broadband, but they're sound and you're half thinking of trying to get a better deal, so you go, '*Maith go leor.* Give me your card anyway.' You can say it as you're walking out the door of your house, or leaving a conversation on the street, or hanging up the phone. It's a universal farewell.

Sláinte agus fad saoil 'ad
Health and long life to you

[slaan-tcha ah-gus fawd sail att]

Ardaigh na gloineacha don lánúin nuaphósta. Sláinte agus fad saoil agaibh.
Raise your glasses to the newly married couple. Health and long life to ye both.

The first cheers of the night among friends

Irish people are fixated with knowing how to say 'cheers' in every language under the sun. We'll raise a glass in the pub after two weeks in Spain and say, '*Salud*, as they say in Malaga.' But there are loads of different ways to say 'cheers' in the Irish language. *'Sláinte agus fad saoil 'ad'* is one of my favourites, and it's commonly used in Ráth Chairn in Meath and Connemara when raising a drink to one's health or one's achievements. You can say *'sláinte'* when you're in the company of many and you want to have a quick 'cheers', but if it's a good session and you want to get a little bit deeper, 'Health and long life to you' is perfect. It sounds like it's been passed down as a blessing from the older generations of Irish-speakers. The most important 'cheers' of all is when you've got your friends in the local pub, the fire's on, you've got a lovely round of stout, and the craic is good. *'Sláinte agus fad saoil 'ad'* is the first cheers of the night among friends. There's no need for anything more. You wish each other good health, take a good slug of your pint, and let the conversation evolve.

Go mbeirimid beo ag an am seo arís
May we be alive here in the same moment next year/Good health, until the same time next year

[guh mer-ra-mwij byo egg on awm shuh ar-eesh]

Right, cé atá ag iarriadh deoch? Sláinte, agus go mbeirimid beo ag an am seo arís.
Right, who wants a drink? Good health to ye, until the same time next year.

> *To wish us all well for the next 12 months.*

I used to say this phrase all the time at the beginning of the *Three Pints* podcast I did with Tommy and Laurita. We would go to little lost country pubs, sit in the snugs, and just let the conversation flow. When the boss came down with the three pints for us at 11 o'clock in the morning, and I'd look at the lovely Guinness and lift it up, and Tommy and Laurita would say *'Sláinte'*, I would always follow with *'Go mbeirimid beo ag an am seo arís.'* May we all be here the same time next year.

It's an important one for me, because I learned it from my mother. She was a west of Ireland woman who had a love for Irish but couldn't speak it. From my first memory of Christmas, I can see her saying, *'Go mbeirimid beo ag an am seo arís'* as she raised her glass of Pedrotti, the classic wine of '80s Ireland. The dinner was cooked, she was the last person to sit down at the table, and she was happy that our family were all there. She only said this phrase once a year in this exact situation to wish us all well for the next 12 months.

Teach gan cíos 'ad
House with no rent to you

[tchyok gone kee-us att]

Íosa, a Bhriain, ní fhaca me le fada an lá thú. Sláinte agus teach gan cíos agat!
Jesus, Brian, it's been way too long. Good health and a house with no rent to ya!

*A phrase born from
the existence of landlords.*

There should be a statue of the person who came up with this phrase put up in the middle of the country. We talk about accommodation and rent so much in Ireland because of the utter quagmire we've found ourselves in when it comes to housing. And here's someone way back when in Connemara coming up with this phrase that still hits a nerve. It shows you that a house with no rent was as important and almost unimaginable back in the 1800s, when a landlord was in charge of your cottage, as it is today, when you're trying to find an apartment. And we're all familiar with the image of an Irish eviction from our secondary-school history books. This is a problem that has been happening in Ireland for centuries, from the plantations to the Famine to the housing crisis. It is a phrase born from the existence of landlords, an ancient blessing with modern connotations.

Bean ar do mhian 'ad
Whatever woman you want

[ban duh duh vee-an att]

Sláinte!
Agus bean ar do mhian 'ad!
Arach, stop, a Briain! A mhac, tá tú ólta.
Good health!
And any woman ya want!
Arra, stop, Brian! You're drunk.

The more pints you have, the more phrases are added on to the sláintes.

This phrase comes down to pure 'cheers' development in Connemara. The more pints you have, the more phrases are added on to the *sláinte*s. You're deep into the session at this stage, another round is put in front of you, you say 'cheers' and someone chimes in with *'Bean ar do mhian 'ad!'* – 'and whatever woman you want!' There's nothing but giddiness at this stage. There's sincerity to *'Sláinte agus fad saoil 'ad'* (page 40), but *'Bean ar do mhian 'ad'* is all about the craic that goes on in an Irish pub. There could be an aul fella sitting at the bar in Galway in his muddy wellies, then the local funny lad in the corner pipes up with *'Bean ar do mhian 'ad!'*, and the aul fella comes back with 'Give me Bo Derek walking out of the ocean in her bikini with her revolver any day!' If you would prefer James Bond himself, you can say, *'Fear ar do mhian 'ad'* as well. Whatever man you want.

Páiste gach bliain 'ad ón mbliain seo amach

A child every year from now on for you

[pawsh-ta gakh blee-an att own mlee-an shuh amok]

Sláinte!
Agus páiste gach bliain 'ad ón mbliain seo amach!
Tá tú ag tógáil an mickey anois, a Bhriain. Tá an iomarca ólta agat, tá sé in am dhul abhaile, a mhac.
Cheers!
And a child every year to ya from now on!
You're taking the piss now, Brian. You've had way too much to drink, go home outta that.

> *You're in a session now, and the sláintes are getting ridiculous.*

You're in with a good crowd, you're four pints in, and everything you were going to do for that day has fallen by the wayside. Dinner is gone out the window and you've already texted the babysitter. You're in a session now, and the *sláinte*s are getting ridiculous. *'Páiste gach bliain 'ad ón mbliain seo amach'* probably harks back to when huge families were seen as a blessing. You have to take your hat off to the mothers and fathers with big families, especially the mighty Irish mothers who had 10 or 12 children or more. These big families were nurtured and reared on next to nothing. Nowadays, if you're sitting in The Glimmer Man in Stoneybatter or Garavan's Bar in Galway City after watching the All-Ireland senior hurling final, another round lands on the table, and you lift your glass and say, 'And a child every year from now on to you!', the whole pub would come to a standstill. People would think you're off your rocker. But it is a very old turn of phrase, and it's a great one to get a reaction when the pints are escalating.

Gob fliuch agus bás in Éirinn
A wet mouth and to die in Ireland

[gub fluck aw-gus baws in air-in]

Sláinte!
Go dtí an chéad uair eile a bheas tú sa mbaile.
Gob fliuch agus bás in Éirinn.
Good health to ya!
Till the next time you're back home again.
A wet mouth and to die in Ireland.

It's one for the diaspora posse.

May your mouth never be dry because it's full of porter! This phrase would have a resonance for the Connemara people who emigrated in the nineteenth and twentieth centuries to Boston and New York, London and Manchester. I'm sure this was said many a time in those cities by people who went to find a better life and knew they might never return to Ireland. It creates an image of those people sitting in a pub in a far-flung place, dreaming of being back home in Connemara, down by the slip and looking at the ocean.

Through doing the podcast, we've had loads of emails from people who have been living undocumented in America for thirty or forty years, saying that our show has made them feel Irish again for the first time in a long time. And these people have no way of getting home for a funeral or a visit because getting in and out of the country would be a nightmare. It sounds like an '80s problem, but there are still thousands of Irish–Americans in this situation.

It's no wonder there are so many songs in Connemara about people who had to emigrate. There's a real poignancy to this phrase. It's one for the diaspora posse.

Go n-éirí an t-ádh leat, go n-éirí an grá leat, má éiríonn an dá rud leat, beidh leat!
Good luck to you, best of luck in love to you, if you get both of those, you're sorted!

[gu neye-ree on taw lat, guh neye-ree on graw lat, ma heye-reen an daw rud lat by lat]

Slán, a Mham. Slán, a Dhaid.
Slán, loveen.
Tabhair aire duit féin amuigh ann.
Cinnte.
Go n-éirí an t-ádh leat, go n-éirí an grá leat, má éiríonn an dá rud leat beidh leat!
Dad, le do thoil …
Bye, Mam. Bye, Dad.
Bye, loveen.
Mind yourself over there.
For sure.
Good luck to you, best of luck in love to you, if you get both of those, you're sorted!
Dad, please …

*If you have luck and you have love,
what more do you want?*

This is like a little poem. The three lines go together so well that they hardly make sense apart. The final line, '*Má éiríonn an dá rud leat, beidh leat!*' doesn't translate well into English, but the sentiment comes down to 'If you get those two, you'll be fine'. You might use this when you're waving someone off who you know you won't see for a while. When your sister and brother-in-law and their five kids are heading back to Clonakilty after staying with you for Christmas, or when parents are saying goodbye to their daughter as she goes through the security at Dublin Airport. It's not a phrase that you would use in normal, everyday conversation. It's more like an Irish haiku, wishing the best to someone. If you have luck and you have love, what more do you want?

TWO

Words to take you on an adventure

It's hard to imagine that my key to the world has been the Irish language. It's brought me to ice roads in Siberia, paddy fields in the Philippines, and deep into the jungles of Honduras. I could never have hoped when I started presenting the travel show on TG4 that I would still be heading off on adventures all over the world 23 years later. After over two decades of exploring and having banter with the locals wherever I find myself, I have built up my vocabulary. I have my go-to words to describe what I'm seeing, who I'm meeting, and what I think about it all. I even have my own catchphrase at this stage: *'Meas mór ag dul amach ...'*, 'Respect to ...' (page 56).

But I'm always trying to keep things fresh and cool, so I've been adding to my arsenal over the years. New places inspire new feelings, so I find new ways in Irish to talk about how *dochreidte* (unreal) something is for all the people sitting in their armchairs at home in Ireland. These are my favourite phrases that I pack in my luggage every time I head off *ag taisteal* (travelling). I hope you find a few you like and take them with you on your adventures as well, whether it's to Leitrim, Lanzarote, or Lagos.

Meas mór ag dul amach go dtí an posse
Respect to my posse

[mass more egg dull a-mock guh djee on posse]

Meas mór ag dul amach go dtí an Navan posseeee!
Shout-out to all the Navan posseeee!

Showing and giving respect Navan style, street-wide and street-wise.

I've been filming my travel show on TG4 for 23 years now. It's bonkers when you think about it. How many other shows last that long on Irish television? And this is on our national language TV station!

We went to America for the first ever series on TG4. It was 2000, and I was about to spend the next four weeks travelling throughout the country to Boston, Chicago and Dallas. I wanted to make the show sound different or cooler in a way, and try to put my stamp on it. So I decided to come up with my very own catchphrase, and what better way to do that than put a twist on an all-American phrase used by the hip-hop lads of the '90s, from Cypress Hill to the Wu-Tang Clan and Dr Dre: 'This is a shout-out to my homies'? And there it was born: '*Meas mór ag dul amach ...*', showing and giving respect Navan style, street-wide and street-wise. I've used it for the last 23 years, and I just signed off my latest series on a remote South Pacific island with it. You know something works when there's a sketch about it on *Gift Grub* on the radio, or a lad in a van outside Centra shouts it out the window at you. So to all of you who are reading this paragraph at this moment in time, *meas mór ag dul amach go dtí an leabhar* posseeeeeee!

Ar bís
Buzzing

[air beesh]

Bhí mé ar bís ag an aerfort.
I was buzzing at the airport.

The feeling of endorphins coursing through your body when you're excited about something.

To be *'ar bís'* is that feeling you get when you're at Dublin Airport, you've got all your new gear on, your passport in your hand, and you're ready to take off on an adventure. It's the feeling of endorphins coursing through your body when you're excited about something. For me, it always happens when I get to travel to some amazing place, like the Amazon or Victoria Falls or the jungle in southern Ethiopia. I know I'm going to make a good TV show just from the beauty of the places, so I'm *ar bís*.

I'd always wanted to see the Grand Canyon. I'd only ever seen it in those yellow *National Geographic* magazines in dentists' or doctors' waiting rooms, and I had all these images in my head, but being there for the TV show was completely different. It was already spectacular enough, but then our local fixer said he was going to bring me to an even more special place with an even more special view. We walked towards a ledge about sixty yards away from the crew, and I saw this expanse in front of me. I was in awe. I had to sit down on my own on a rock and take all of it in. It was almost too hard for my eyes to accept. I was sitting beside this humongous piece of Mother Nature, over 270 miles long, the Colorado River meandering down into its belly, sphinx-like patterns and temple-like shapes catching me off guard. I nearly started crying with the beauty. *Bhí mé ar bís* to finally see it in person.

Fuinneamh
Energy

[fwin-yav]

Bhí fuinneamh iontach sa seomra an lá sin.
There was great energy in the room that day.

My zest for life.

I'm not sure where we get our *fuinneamh* from, but we love wondering about it: 'WHERE does she get her energy from?' It's a powerful word for me – even the pronunciation is powerful. *'Fuinneamh'* sounds like it's coming up from the ground, like a spring from deep in a mountain. I've been blessed to have *fuinneamh* in my career and in my life, and I suppose it comes from the people around me. That's my zest for life. My wife, my sons, my brothers on the road, Rosco and Evan, whom I've worked with for over 23 years on TG4. I got *fuinneamh* in the Hen House with Tommy and Laurita on the podcast.

I truly believe if you can surround yourself with the people you like, the people you get and the people who get you, then a little more of everything can be achieved. When my brother, Freddy, died suddenly a few summers ago, I retreated out into my garden for weeks. There the land, the grass, the trees, the bees, the sky, the birds, the sun, the clouds, the rain all gave me *fuinneamh* when I needed it most. You might get it from nature, from your family, from sports or from music, but when you find it, make sure to absorb it.

An timpeallacht
The environment

[on teem-pell-okt]

Is breá liom an timpeallacht atá mórthimpeall orm:
Gaillimh, an fharraige, na daoine, an chathair, iarthar na hÉireann.
I love the environment that surrounds me:
Galway, the sea, the people, the city, the west of Ireland.

*Everything in your vicinity,
and it could be good or bad.*

I've travelled the world in HiAce vans. Every time we arrive at an airport, whether it's Siberia or Bangkok, Ethiopia or Nicaragua, there's a HiAce van waiting for us. They can be basic or souped-up, with curtains and water holders, but you should never underestimate the power of a HiAce.

Those first couple of days in a new place, I'm taking in the environment through the window of the van. I could be passing the lush forests of Papua New Guinea with nothing but trees around me, or I could be whizzing through Dhaka in Bangladesh and see a guy with six washing machines on the back of a rickshaw. The window is my snapshot of life and I try to absorb it all. What am I seeing, how am I feeling, and what am I going to say about it? We usually spend eight days in a single country and from that we get a one-hour TV show, so I've got to let the place fill my head and not shy away from what I might be thinking about it.

An timpelleacht is everything in your vicinity, and it could be good or bad. It's the trees, it's the sky, it's your estate, it's your road, it's your house, it's your people.

Go forleathan
Widespread

[guh for-la-han]

Gan aon dabht, bhí corned beef *in úsáid go forleathan sna boscaí lóin sna hochtóidí san Uaimh.*
Without a doubt, the use of corned beef in sandwiches was widespread in lunch boxes in Navan during the '80s.

Always makes me think of the little green nut in Papua New Guinea that's chewed by everyone.

'*Go forleathan*' means widespread, something that is absolutely everywhere. So you could say COVID was *go forleathan* for the last few years. It's a word I use when I'm 10,000 kilometres away on my travels and I'm trying to conjure up an image for viewers at home.

The phrase always makes me think of the little green nut in Papua New Guinea that's chewed by everyone. It's called the betel nut, and every man, woman and even youngster uses it. It suppresses hunger, it's a source of energy, and it gives people a buzz. If you're driving a taxi or a bus, or you're just heading to work or walking miles to school, you chew it. The locals carry a small bag with all they need for the day inside: 10 to 15 fresh betel nuts, a packet of calcium powder made from coral, and some small mustard plants. They dip these into the powder and it all mixes in the mouth with the betel nut to create the most vivid blood-red saliva. It stains their mouths and rots their teeth, but in a place with little money and even less food, *tá an* betel nut *in úsáid go forleathan* (the use of the betel nut is widespread).

Dochreidte
Unreal

[duh-crej-ha]

Tá an radharc sin dochreidte!
That view is unreal!

When something is simply outstanding.

In Navan we used to say 'vintage' when something was really good, and *'dochreidte'* reminds me of that. It's for when something is simply outstanding. I probably used this word a hundred times in my first ever travel show as a young red-headed Navan man landing in the US. I thought absolutely everything was *dochreidte*. And then I went to the Amazon ...

We had travelled down from French Guiana into Brazil and landed in the city of Manaus. That was the first time I saw the waters of the Amazon. We journeyed by boat up the mighty Rio Negro and pods of pink river dolphins joined us as we went deeper and deeper into this liquid jungle. There were supermarkets with mobile petrol pumps sitting on the river, busy with passing boats stopping to fill up, like floating Applegreens. It was ... *bhuel, bhí sé dochreidte!*

But you don't have to be in the Amazon to use it. You could be on a beach in Donegal, in the valleys of Glendalough, or driving through your town on a Friday afternoon and the county council have decided to rip up most of Main Street. Its uses are boundless.

Damanta
Unreal
[da-mawn-ta]

Bhí an bháisteach agus an ghaoth damanta aréir i nGaillimh.
The rain and wind were unreal last night in Galway.

A great word for an almighty headache, a terrible hangover, woeful karaoke, or a shite wedding.

Unlike '*dochreidte*' (page 66), '*damanta*' has a bit of negativity to it. There's pain involved in the word. It's brilliant for a shite situation. You can see Teresa Mannion standing at a roundabout in Salthill getting hammered by a gale, seawater flowing down her face, saying the weather is *damanta* so don't make any unnecessary journeys.

We have plenty of opportunities to use this one during winter when the rain and the wind hit. You arrive back from work in the middle of January and all you can say is, 'Jesus, you wouldn't believe the weather. *Tá sé damanta.*' You can use it to describe the physical body and undesirable situations as well, so it's a great word for an almighty headache, a terrible hangover, woeful karaoke, or a shite wedding. It's a really strong adjective for when something is Teresa Mannion levels of awful.

Ar mo sháimhín só
Chilled out/relaxed

[air muh haw-veen so]

Is breá liom an t-am sin den tráthnona, an dinnéar thart, an meaisín gréithre lán, an tine lasta, agus Champions League *ar an mbosca ... ar mo sháimhín só.*
I love that time of the evening when the dinner's over, the dishwasher is full, the fire's on, and *Champions League* is on the telly ... chilled out.

A beautiful, melodic way to say that you're chilled out.

This is a beautiful, melodic way to say that you're chilled out. There's an intonation in the way it is pronounced, almost like it swings: 'err muh HAW-veen ho'. And you can't rush this phrase either; you have to take your time with it. The feeling and meaning of the phrase is embedded in how you say it.

To be *ar do sháimhín só*, you need to be relaxing on a tropical island, watching the sunset, your hammock gently swinging. Or you could be at home by the fire, with the couch all to yourself and a cup of tea in your hand. The dishwasher's done and the kids are in bed, and you've got your favourite show on. No distractions, you're just snug as a bug in a rug. This phrase says everything about having a nice level of contentment, no matter where you are. It's a state of mind, like you're The Dude in *The Big Lebowski* walking around in your dressing gown with a White Russian in your hand.

Cuireann sé soir mé
It does my head in

[cur-ren shay serr may]

Is fuath liom nuair a bhíonn daoine ag tabhairt amach faoin tír seo an t-am ar fad, cuireann sé soir mé.
I can't stand listening to people give out all the time about this country, it does my head in.

> *Even the English version, 'it does my head in', is hard to explain.*

This is a phrase from deepest Connemara that I've brought with me to the other side of the world. Even the English version, 'it does my head in', is hard to explain. How do you teach that to a Spanish student? But that's the beauty of the language, and we love the phrase. I can guarantee you somebody somewhere in the space of you reading this will have said, 'It/she/he does my head in.'

I got caught out big time live on national radio a few years ago when I was filling in for Ian Dempsey on his breakfast show. It was around half eight on a Friday morning, the show was flying along, and we had just gone to an ad break. I asked one of the producers what song was up after the ads and they said it was Ellie Goulding. 'Ahh Jaysus, not Ellie Goulding,' I said, 'she does my head in.' Within seconds the screen lit up with texts as hundreds of people from all over the country told me that my microphone was still live. Some of the listeners said it was the funniest piece of radio they'd heard in years. Now, I have nothing against Ellie Goulding, my feelings are completely irrational, but *cuireann sí soir mé*. So *anois* in honour of the great Ellie Goulding.

Déistineach
Disgusting

[day-shta-nock]

Is cuimhin liom a bheith i margadh torthaí in Phnom Penh uair amháin. Thóg mé suas an durian, bhí boladh déistineach uaidh, ar nós stocaí lofa, ach is breá le muintir na háite iad.

I remember being in a fruit market in Phnom Penh once. I picked up the durian fruit, it smelt absolutely disgusting, like rotten socks, but the locals love them.

The lingering odour of a stranger ...

I've stayed in a fair few places over the years while away, some nice, some not so nice, and some downright *déistineach*. I hope to at least have a clean pillowcase and sheet on the bed, but if I can't even have that much, no matter where I am, I will adapt. I will stuff the pillow into a T-shirt so I can smell myself instead of the lingering odour of a stranger. Once I had to sleep in a B&B in the very north of Scotland. It was a freezing and damp aul January. We only finished work at 11 o'clock at night, so we had a key to get into the B&B we had booked. There was a distinct fusty damp smell in the downstairs hallway. I made my way to my room, opened the door, and there was a cat on my bed. Just sitting there, looking at me as if to say, 'What are you doing in here?' After getting rid of the cat, I checked the bed and found stains and hairs on the sheets ... and the hairs didn't belong to the cat. So I adapted. I slept on the floor beside a small blow heater that I found in the fusty old wardrobe. *Bhí sé déistineach!*

Ag tumadh isteach ...
Diving in ...

[egg tuh-ma ish-tock]

An bealach is fearr le teanga a fhoghlaim ná tú féin a thumadh i gcultúr na háite.
The best way to learn a language is to dive deep into the culture of the place.

I love to use it when talking about immersing myself in a new culture, a new place or a new language.

To 'dive in' to a culture is to fully immerse yourself. I've been to the Omo Valley in southern Ethiopia twice. It's a 10-hour drive from Addis Ababa. It's where the southern tribes live: the Hamar, the Mursi and the Banna. In Ireland, what comes to mind when we think of Ethiopia might be drought, famine and Live Aid, but the south of Ethiopia is lush and green. There are lakes and mountains and waterfalls and blue skies. It's one of the richest, most diverse places I've ever been to in terms of colours, traditions and language, and their customs are as strong as ever. So I had to dive in to experience it.

It's the same with language – you have to commit and surround yourself with it to fully learn it. It's why going to the Gaeltacht when you're in school adds to your ability to speak Irish. I learned how to speak Spanish because I moved to Bilbao and lived with other people who didn't have a word of English. I had no choice but to *tumadh isteach* if I wanted to get by. Now, you can use this phrase for 'diving in' to the sea at six o'clock in the morning at Salthill, but I love to use it when talking about immersing myself in a new culture, a new place, or a new language.

Gafa
Busy

[gof-fa]

Ghlaoigh mé ar an tiler *inné. Dúirt sé liom teacht ar ais aige i gceann sé mhí, théis na Nollag. Tá sé gafa, a dúirt sé.*
I called the tiler yesterday. He said to come back to him in six months, after the Christmas. He said he's flat out altogether.

> *You don't even have time to make a sandwich or go to the toilet, you're that busy.*

You're up the walls, out the door, up to your eyeballs, snowed under, *tá tú gafa*. You don't even have time to make a sandwich or go to the toilet, you're that busy. This is what happens when you call a tradesperson in Ireland, whether a tiler, a plumber, a builder, or an electrician: '*Tá mé gafa*. I might be able to fit you in next year.' You could have Niagara Falls coming out of your toilet and the plumber will still tell you they won't be able to get to you until after Christmas.

'*Gafa*' also means obsessed, which adds an extra level to it. You could say you're *gafa* with Daniel O'Donnell or *Game of Thrones*. But when it comes to busyness, '*gafa*' really paints a picture – it's an engaged tone in word form. 'Sorry, Mam, I can't talk now. I'm making a chorizo risotto. *Tá mé gafa*.'

Ag moilliú síos
Slowing down

[egg mwill-ah shee-us]

Thóg sé seachtain orm moilliú síos go luas an oileáin.
It took me a week to slow down to the pace of the island.

I prefer to use this phrase as a sense of being, to 'wind down'.

I've used this phrase all over the world, from Inis Meáin off the west coast of Ireland to the village of Tulagi in the Solomon Islands.

You can use *'ag moilliú síos'* in a literal sense too, so you might be *'ag moilliú síos'* if you're driving on the motorway and you see a speed van. I know the road to Dublin inside out. I swear to God, I think the car knows how to get to Dublin and back on the motorway without me. I can pinpoint where the speed vans on the road to Dublin will be, so I always know when to slow down.

But I prefer to use this phrase as a sense of being, to 'wind down'. Like a shift of gears in life. You slow down after a mental day at work or when you head off on holiday. Your body clock takes time off and you eventually match the pace of the place you find yourself.

Dáiríre píre
Really and truly/very serious about something

[dah-rir-ah pir-ah]

*Chuala mé gur bhuaigh sé an Lotto Dé Sathairn
le Quick Pick €2.
Dairíre píre?*
I heard he won the Lotto on Saturday with
a €2 Quick Pick!
Are you kidding me?

Probably used most often as an answer to a question.

This phrase has to be one of the more fun things to say in Irish. It has a lovely, sing-songy pronunciation. You could almost have a cartoon character called Dáirire Píre – the Irish version of Dora the Explorer. It is probably used most often as an answer to a question. 'Did you hear Séamus won the Lotto?' 'What? *Dáirire píre?*' It's like saying, 'You're messing! You're joking!' It's a brilliant phrase for exciting news.

I did my first audition for TG4 in October 1996. There were loads of people sitting in the waiting room of this tiny studio to try out for a brand-new TV station. I went into the audition room and they gave me a box. The idea was that I had to talk to camera about whatever was in the box for three minutes and try to sound as natural as possible. It was a bottle of suntan lotion. And here I am, a redhead covered in freckles – definitely not built for the sun.

A few days later, I got a call on my massive cement block of a phone – I was like Dom Joly if he lived in a tiny flat in Galway and was getting rent allowance. It was TG4 saying I got the job. I was incredulous. I turned to Dympna and told her the news. '*Dáirire?*' she said. '*Dáirire píre!*' I answered, and we jumped around the kitchen. So this phrase has been with me from the beginning, even though the job lasted for six months and I was straight back on the dole.

Luas agus rithim na háite
The speed and rhythm of the place

[loo-ass aw-guss ri-him naa haw-tcha]

Tógann sé cúpla lá ort dul i dtaithí ar luas agus rithim na háite.
It takes a few days to get used to the rhythm and pace of the place.

You can feel it coming from the buildings, the traffic, the people.

I like to use *'luas agus rithim na háite'* every time I'm in a major city. It could be Bangkok or Tokyo. You know when there's fifteen or sixteen million people living in a city that there's going to be a buzz about it. When you arrive in Jakarta or Ho Chi Minh and there are millions of mopeds, trucks and vans, and they're all honking their horns, you will find the beating heart of the place beneath the sounds of chaos. You can feel the *luas agus rithim* coming from the buildings, the traffic, the people. There's movement everywhere. Imagine heading from Longford to Los Angeles and you get to experience that frenetic pace of a humongous city for the first time. You can say *'ag moilliú síos'* (page 80) when you need to slow down, and *'luas agus rithim na háite'* when you have to keep up.

Níos doimhní san aistear
Deeper into the adventure

[nees dye-nee san ash-ter]

Táimid níos doimhní san aistear anois ná mar a bhíomar ariamh.
We are deeper into the adventure now than we have ever been.

When we're going off the beaten track, heading deeper into a new territory.

When I started having my travel adventures, I didn't know the word 'aistear'. It's only appeared on my horizon in the past five or so years, but now that I know it, I use it regularly. That's something I love about a language: you can be speaking it for years, find a new word, and it brings a freshness to it.

When I say *'níos doimhní san aistear'*, it feels like I have a map in my hand. We use maps all the time on my travel show, to navigate and to show the viewers where we're off to. I have an old Irish AA road atlas in my car that I bought 20 years ago from a petrol station just across the road from the Bulmers cider factory in Clonmel. It's battered and bruised, and there are pages missing, but I like taking it out and looking at the county I'm in and seeing where I'm going.

'Aistear' feels like you're pushing the boundaries of travel, and it's amazing that I'd been having loads of adventures for years on the TV show and I didn't know the word for it. I use it now when we're going off the beaten track, heading deeper into a new territory. But you don't have to be Tom Crean to use it; your *aistear* could be in a campervan or on a Ryanair flight, or it could be a journey of the mind through a story that you want to know more about – it doesn't matter, it's about exploration.

Cinéaltacht agus cneastacht
Kindness and warmth

[kin-all-tockt aw-guss kin-ass-tockt]

Thaispeáin muintir na háite cinéaltacht agus cneastacht dhochreidte dúinn ó leaindeáil muid.
The locals have shown us an amazing level of kindness since we have arrived.

> *I've met the happiest people who are living on a dollar a day.*

I'm most definitely a people person. I'm happiest when I'm sitting at the side of the road in Indonesia with somebody trying to sell something, or in Khartoum with someone who's making me a cup of local red tea. There's not a word of English spoken and I just let the moment breathe. I've met the happiest people who are living on a dollar a day; they might not have much, but they greet you with *cineáltacht agus cneastacht*.

When we visited Khartoum in Sudan a few years ago, it was just after the revolution. It is the most amazing city on the banks of the Nile, where the White Nile meets the Blue Nile. I was fascinated with the person who sings the call to prayer, and I wanted to do a story in a mosque. So I went to the leader of the mosque, the Sheikh, who was the richest man in the area, and asked, 'Can I see the person who sings the call to prayer that hits the loudspeaker outside and goes all over the neighbourhood?' The Sheikh had built the mosque and he and his family invited me in with open arms. There must have been about five hundred people in the mosque, and all the elders came and shook my hand and I felt their kindness. They were fascinated about Ireland, and they offered me tea and were hugging me and everything. After that I went to the Sheikh's home and the family took me in and made me the most delicious Sudanese food. I spent an amazing day with them. They showed me a level of *cineáltacht agus cneastacht* I'd never experienced from strangers before.

Muintir na háite
The locals

[mwin-ter na haw-tcha]

Ó Inis Meáin go Addis Ababa, 'siad muintir na háite is tábhachtaí.
From Inis Meáin to Addis Ababa, it's the locals who are the most important.

You might take them for granted, but the people are what make a place.

The most important people in the world are the locals. It doesn't matter if you are in Navan or Addis Ababa; if you get in with the locals, you're flying. You meet them every day in the butcher's, the supermarket, the football pitch, the coffee shop. When I'm away travelling, we make the best TV with the locals. They know what's what and they have the best stories. And when I get home to Galway, I'm straight back into the fluency of my neighbourhood, and my local butcher nearly always says, 'Hector, I haven't seen you in weeks. Were you out foreign?' I was, but I was hanging out with the locals.

If you think about it, we even call the closest pub in our area 'the local', because it's that important to us. It's where we meet our neighbours, the ordinary people of the parish who we see every day. And you might take them for granted, but the people are what make a place. Even *'muintir na háite'* literally translates as 'the people of the place'. It's a bit of a Ronseal phrase, but it does the job nicely.

Ag/ar deireadh thiar thall
At the end of the day/When all is said and done

[egg/air djer-ra hear hall]

Ar deireadh thiar thall, tá Craobh na hÉireann buaite ag Maigh Eo!
At last, Mayo have won the All-Ireland championship!

Real sports commentator talk that brings everyone back into focus.

When you're at the committee meeting in the local clubhouse or the parents' association AGM has gone into its third hour, and someone is going on and on and on ... you can say, 'Look, we can talk all day, but when all is said and done, if we're going to win the county championship, we have to pull the finger out and make a commitment.' It's real sports commentator talk that brings everyone back into focus. You'll have Coach O'Brien bamboozling 12-year-olds with all the lingo: 'Johnny, you have to mark the centre forward. Pat, you know what you have to do. We're going to move this ball a lot quicker, lads. It's what we've been training for: off the shoulder, hand pass, and when the kick is on, lads, use it.' And then he sees all the blank faces looking up at him and goes, '*Ag deireadh thiar thall*, lads, it's up to you.'

THREE

Emotional words for every mood

We have an emotion for every day of the year in Ireland. I don't know of any other nationality in the world that reacts to the way the week shapes up for them like Irish people do. You could be *dubh dóite* (fed up, page 116) on a Monday and full of *ríméad* (giddiness, page 96) by Wednesday because you know the weekend is coming. It could be freezing and stormy out, but the whole country is buoyant because it's a bank holiday weekend.

It's like the people who call into Joe Duffy's *Liveline* radio show. All they do is give out about stuff. It's contagious. We don't celebrate being happy often enough because it's not newsworthy. I was talking about this on the *THL* podcast and they joked that we should have a positive version of *Liveline* and I should host it. Listeners calling in to share their positive outlook on life. Wouldn't that be brilliant?

I'd like to say there's a word for every feeling in this chapter but that's not true. I noticed that the words I'm drawn to most in Irish to describe emotions are happy words, and even the ones that deal with difficult feelings have their own beauty. And there's room for merriment as well, so I've put in what I like to call the Dual Carriageway of Intoxication (page 133).

We can't be positive all the time, and sometimes I'm too *spíonta* (shattered, page 98) to leave the house, but if you open yourself up to it, there are little happiness epiphanies there for you every day: all you have to do is see them. And then you can call me on *Positive Liveline*. Talk to Hector: 51559. The line is open.

Sona sásta, gliondar, ríméad
Blissful, a happy heart, giddiness

[sun-na saws-ta, glun-der, reem-aid]

Tá mé sona sasta.
I'm so happy/absolutely thrilled.

Tá gliondar mór a chroí aige.
He's got a big heart.

Bhí ríméad orainn ag dul go Stradbally don Picnic.
We were all giddy heading to Stradbally for the Picnic.

The Holy Trinity of inner contentment.

This is the Holy Trinity of inner contentment. There are so many ways to say you are happy in Irish, which makes you realise that we are a happy tribe. We say we're happy through our culture, our chat, our songs and dances. We've been happy for millennia, and we've found loads of ways to express our joy.

'*Sásta*' means happy, but '*sona sásta*'? You are super happy. Absolutely DELIGHTED. You have a contentment about you.

'*Gliondar*' means you're happy in your heart. When you say someone has '*gliondar*', it's as if they're shining from within themselves. You can imagine a gorgeous glow on their face; '*gliondar*' even sounds like 'glow' or 'glister'.

'*Ríméad*' means there's a giddiness in you, you're happy-go-lucky. I love '*ríméad*' because I get a lot of giddy feelings, and I think we should hold on to that as we get older. I was incredibly giddy in school, always laughing with Tommy when he was sitting beside me in first year in secondary school. We became great friends and we're still giddy and laughing like we did when we were teenagers. When I was recording the podcast with Tommy and Laurita, *bhí ríméad orm* the minute I walked into the Hen House, because I knew we were going to have fun, and I knew we were going to go down different roads of conversation and we were going to laugh. I was guaranteed to leave feeling *sona sásta* after a good aul *ríméad* podcast session.

Spíonta
Shattered

[spee-un-ta]

Tháinig an t-eitleán isteach ag a ceathair a chlog ar maidin, bhí orm tiomáint ansin go Ciarraí, bhí mé spíonta faoin am a shroich mé Farranfore.
The flight got in at 4 a.m., I had to drive then to Kerry, I was shattered by the time I got to Farranfore.

When both body and mind are exhausted.

'*Spíonta*' is for when both body and mind are exhausted. Your eyes are half closed and you don't know whether you're coming or going. For me it describes the feeling of driving down to Clare when my two lads were babies to collect them from the in-laws after Mammy and Daddy had spent three days and three nights at Electric Picnic. I have done my fair share of festivals, but I'd never had to return to a one-year-old and a two-year-old before. We didn't leave the Body & Soul area till late the night before so it felt like our souls left our bodies the morning after. All we could think about was the *leaba*.

At the best of times, it's how most people feel on a Monday morning heading into work, after being away for the weekend or at a wedding that went on for three days. I can almost see people yawning and rubbing their eyes when I say '*spíonta*'. Absolutely shattered.

Scriosta
Destroyed

[shkrish-ta]

Théis trí lá a chaitheamh in Stradbally ag an Electric Picnic, bhí mé scriosta ag dul abhaile ar an Luan.
After three days at the Electric Picnic in Stradbally, I was destroyed going home on the Monday.

On the scale of being wrecked, it's a 10 out of 10.

'*Scriosta*' is the best friend of '*spíonta*' (page 98). It literally means to destroy, like when a building is demolished or a bomb destroys a town. So it's a useful word you can use when you're talking about things like the Amazon rainforest being wiped out, but it can also be used to mean you're just really, really tired.

We love talking about being tired in Ireland. It's like the weather: we never stop talking about how unbelievably wrecked we feel. It's the last thing we think of before we go to bed at night and the first thing we think of when we wake up in the morning. You're tired when you get up for work on Monday, you're really tired by Wednesday, and by Friday you're *scriosta*. On the scale of being wrecked, it's a 10 out of 10. It knocks school-level '*tá tuirse orm*' out of the park. There's no way a child should come home from sixth class and fire the schoolbag up on the table and go, '*Jesus Christ, tá mé scriosta.*' You shouldn't even be allowed say this if you're doing the Leaving Cert. '*Scriosta*' is an adult-only word, because being this tired is a rite of passage.

Bailithe
Away in the head

[baw-lee]

Tá sé bailithe.
He is away in the head/cracked.

They're cracked, but in a good way: mad for pints, mad for a laugh, mad for divilment.

This word sums up the DNA of the mad people we all know. They're cracked, but in a good way: mad for pints, mad for a laugh, mad for divilment. My mother would always say, 'Jaysis, he's cracked' about my friends, so I knew I was in good company. It literally means 'gone', so it's a perfect description for someone who is away with the fairies. Its pronunciation is gorgeous: 'BAW-lee'. You can really exaggerate the stress on the 'baw' to make the word even more descriptive.

You can use *'bailithe'* for someone who is completely cuckoo, like Pat Shortt's character in *Father Ted* sitting on the wall in his 'I shot JR' T-shirt, but it's more suited to your friend who's just mad as a brush. They're the extrovert in the group and the night's not the same if they don't come out. Everyone needs a *bailithe* pal in their WhatsApp group. They're the best people to call in to you on a Friday evening, just when you thought you were going to spend the night watching Netflix.

Cantalach

Grumpy

[cawn-ta-lock]

Tá sé chomh cantalach le dris.
He is as cantankerous as a briar.

> *Some people wear their grumpiness as a personality trait, like the prickly aul lad sitting in the corner of the local bar.*

Describing someone as cantankerous as a briar immediately lets you know what type of person they are, there's no doubt about it. You can imagine putting your hand into a briar, and that's how it feels when someone who is *cantalach* aims their grumpiness at you. It's a word heavy with meaning.

I think the world shapes our grumpiness. We've all been the miserable teenager pulled out of bed for the family reunion, or the tired child who throws themselves on the ground in the middle of Granny's birthday party. But some people wear their grumpiness as a personality trait, like the prickly aul lad sitting in the corner of the local bar: the life he's lived and the weather he's seen and the dinners he's eaten and the relationships he's had have made him who he is, and he'll never change.

I moved into my village in Galway 18 years ago, and the aul lads in the local have only started to say hello to me in the past few years. It's taken that long. *Bhí siad cantalach.*

Smut(achán)
A sourpuss

[smut-a-kawn]

Bhí smut ar a aghaidh mar ní raibh sé in ann dul go Cheltenham leis na leaids.
He had a sourpuss on him because he couldn't go to Cheltenham with the boys.

The face on the teenager in the restaurant because the battery on their phone has died.

I know you know that facial expression. It's the look of a child in the supermarket because they can't open the massive pack of Coco Pops while they're sitting in the front of the trolley, or the face on the teenager in the restaurant because the battery on their phone has died. We perfect it as a child and carry it through to adulthood.

My missus can spot me a mile away when I have a puss on my face. I'll sort of lower the jaw a little bit like I'm a six-year-old and she'll go, 'What's wrong with you?' And I'm usually a *smutachán* because I have man flu or I can't go out with the lads because the date clashes with something else.

You wouldn't necessarily say 'sourpuss' in English, but you might say, 'Jaysis, would you look at the head on him.' I'm a great one for saying that on the motorway when someone has been driving up your arse or undertakes you on the hard shoulder. When you finally catch up with them, and you look over to see the face of the person who's been annoying you, they always have a massive *smutachán* head on them.

Ciotach
Awkward

[kyuh-tukh]

Tá stíl chiotach ag an leaid sin ag tógáil na poic shaora, ach déarfaidh mé an méid seo leat, oibríonn sé.
Yer man has an awkward style of taking the Poc Saor, but I tell ya one thing, it works.

Walking into a room full of people you don't know, starting a new job or asking someone out.

There are situations in life where everyone will feel a little bit awkward, whether it's walking into a room full of people you don't know or starting a new job or asking someone out. I used to feel *ciotach* as a red-headed fella growing up, with the slaggings I got from people calling me 'carrot top' and 'Duracell'. I didn't think I was handsome, but then as I got older I got strength from being a confident redhead. I think everyone feels awkward when they're a teenager, but as time goes by, that awkwardness becomes less and less, and with any luck you'll start to feel a bit more *'bainte amach'* (page 162).

It's so interesting that the word for 'awkward' in Irish comes from the same place as the word for left-handed: *'ciotóg'*. It's an echo of that time in Ireland when somebody left-handed was thought of as awkward, or that something was wrong with them. It's embedded in the language. But of course, there's nothing awkward about being left-handed, only that you have to live in a right-handed world.

'Ciotóg' can also mean left-footed, which is an interesting one for sports. We were all right-handers and right-footers in my house in Navan, but my two lads are *ciotógs*. There's something beautiful about a left-footer when they play, the way they address the ball, the way they strike it, and there's nothing *ciotach* about it.

Sceitimíní
Goosebumps

[shketch-eh-mee-nee]

Nuair a tháinig Katie Taylor amach don troid, wow!
Bhí sceitmíní an domhain orm.
When Katie Taylor walked out for the fight, wow!
I was excited.

One thing guaranteed to give me goosebumps is 'Amhrán na bhFiann' being pelted out by 80,000 people in Croke Park or the Aviva.

This is one of the first words I remember picking up in the Gaeltacht, and I use it all the time. It's without doubt one of my favourites. I get *sceitimíní* all the time when I'm filming the travel show, especially when I'm strapped to a microlight with a Briggs & Stratton engine behind me, like a lawnmower with wings, whooshing high over Victoria Falls. But one thing guaranteed to give me goosebumps is 'Amhrán na bhFiann' being pelted out by 80,000 people in Croke Park or the Aviva. There are grown men and women bawling their eyes out, and everyone is singing. I'm a real sucker for national anthems at sporting occasions.

The most iconic moment is John 'The Bull' Hayes crying when Ireland beat England for the first time ever in a rugby match held in Croke Park. I was watching it on TV in my sitting room, and the camera panned across the Irish team and came to The Bull, this big physical specimen of a man from Bruff in County Limerick, and there were tears running down his face. And then I started bawling crying. And then my son Rían, only six at the time, ran into the room and started crying because he thought Daddy was upset. Then my wife ran in: 'What's going on here?' 'Nothing, it's just The Bull Hayes and he's crying.' Then the whole country started bawling crying. That was a real *sceitimíní* moment.

Santach
Greedy

[sawn-tok]

Na creach-chistí sin a cheannaigh/scrios Baile Átha Cliath, anois, sin dream atá santach.
Those vulture funds who have bought up/destroyed Dublin, now, that is a greedy shower.

We've seen greed in the banking crisis, the vulture funds and the landlord renting out a mattress under the stairs for a grand a month.

The way you say this word makes it sound even greedier: 'SAWN-toch'. It's a word to be said with passion and a look of disgust on your face. Ireland has been flooded with *daoine santacha*. We've seen greed in the banking crisis, the vulture funds, and the landlord renting out a mattress under the stairs for a grand a month. It's around every corner, sitting in a brand-new BMW X5 parked at the entrance to a half-finished housing estate.

'Santach' has meaning for every person in every culture. I've seen it on my travels. Greed breeds the world over. There's always the child at the birthday party who takes all the sweets for themselves, but as a parent, you try and instil into your children from the earliest age: 'Don't be greedy. Be kind.' For certain people, though, something changes and they just want more. I hate the word 'greedy' in English, but I do use the word *'santach'*, so I want you to keep this one in your pocket. Thankfully, as much *saint* as there is in life, there's plenty of *flaithiúlacht* (generosity) left on this island.

Scleondar
Buzzing atmosphere

[shclun-der]

Bhí scleondar iontach ag an ngig.
There was an amazing atmosphere at the gig.

A special word for a special happening, when a load of human beings come together and create a groundswell of atmosphere and energy.

'*Scleondar*' is a special word for a special happening, when a load of human beings come together and create a groundswell of atmosphere and energy. There's the murmur before a gig that increases to a buzz, and when the act comes onstage, the atmosphere takes you somewhere.

I've been mad into gigs since I used to go to the SFX and the Olympia in Dublin, and I loved that hum of the crowd waiting for the music to start. I saw Nirvana twice in two weeks in the 1990s. First in Dublin supported by The Breeders and Teenage Fanclub, and then I emigrated to Bilbao and saw them play in the basketball arena a couple of weeks later. The anticipation of getting to see them play live was immense.

Maybe Nirvana aren't your thing, but you might feel a *scleondar* if you're watching your parish compete in the county final. It really describes that connection between a crowd of people all buzzing off each other at an event, because it's the people who create *scleondar*.

Dubh dóite
Fed up/wrecked

[dove doy-tcha]

Tá mé dubh dóite den obair.
I'm fed up with work.

> *That fed up, browned-off feeling when you're trying to get them out of bed to study or do a 'bit' as we say in the Ó hEochagáin household.*

A parent of a teenager will get great use out of this phrase. It's that fed up, browned-off feeling when you're trying to get them out of bed to study, or do a 'bit' as we say in the Ó hEochagáin household. The amount of times myself and my wife, Dympna, have had the same conversation: 'Is he up?' 'Go up there and wake him.'

Getting them to study is one thing, but trying to get teenage lads to flush the toilet after a wee is the greatest bane of our lives. It's eight o'clock on a normal Tuesday night. The teenage son is supposed to be doing a bit of study. Myself and Dympna are watching *The Bear* and we're really into it. The fire's on. We're cosy. Then he goes into the toilet in the hallway, and we can hear him having an absolute horse of a wee. And we're sitting there waiting for the flush: 'Pause it there. Did you hear him flushing the toilet? He's gone off without flushing it again. What age is he? He's left the light on as well.' And then I'm shouting out the door: 'FOR GOD'S SAKE, WILL YOU JUST FLUSH THE TOILET? I'M SICK AND TIRED OF IT. YOU'RE EIGHTEEN YEARS OF AGE WILL YOU JUST LEARN TO FLUSH THE FUCKING TOILET?! Right, press play there.' And it's back to *The Bear*.

'*Dubh dóite*' literally translates as 'burnt black', so it would also be a great phrase to describe that feeling of burnout you get in work, when your energy levels have been cremated. You are truly at the end of your tether if you are *dubh dóite*.

In ísle brí
Down in the dumps/sad

[in eesh-la bree]

Bhí me in ísle brí théis na sochraide, ach buíochas le Dia tá mé i bhfad níos fearr anois.
I was down in the dumps after the funeral, but thank God I'm doing a lot better now.

There's no energy in the body, there's no momentum, you are at a low ebb.

'*In ísle brí*' is a low, flat feeling, like you are at low tide. There's no energy in the body, there's no momentum, you are at a low ebb. There's a beautiful musicality to its pronunciation: 'in EESH-la bree'. It sounds like gentle, small waves rolling into shore.

It literally translates as 'low meaning', so the best way to describe the phrase in English would be 'down in the dumps'. We say it so much in households across Ireland: 'How's Peter doing?' 'Ah, he's a bit down in the dumps.' It's a soft description for a sad feeling. I've been there when my brother died. Every household has felt it. '*In ísle brí*' is a phrase for a tremendously hard time: grief and loss can cause it, and even *as Béarla* it has strength in meaning. But somewhere along the line, the sun rises into a blue sky, the mind lifts, and *ísle brí* fades into the distance.

Níl mé istigh liom féin
Not in with myself/Not in great form

[neel may ish-tee lum hain]

An bhfuil rud éigin mícheart le Seán? Níl sé istigh leis féin in aon chor.
Is there something wrong with Seán? He isn't his usual self at all.

> *There could be anything wrong with them, from a pet dying to them just having an off day, but you know something's not quite right.*

We are masters of understatement in this country, like when we say someone 'isn't themselves'. There could be anything wrong with them, from a pet dying to them just having an off day, but you know something's not quite right.

I was one of the first guests on the *Late Late Show* when Patrick Kielty took over. I was there with Tommy and Laurita, and everything that could have gone wrong went wrong. I was sitting so close to Patrick Kielty that I was practically on his lap. I could see he was nervous, and those nerves spread over to me. And then he asked me a question straight out of the gates that we had prepared for to come at the end.

'Hector, you're back on the road. Papua New Guinea and South-East Asia.'

'I am, yeah. South-East Asia.'

I didn't open my mouth for the rest of the interview. Over a million people tuned in and I just sat there like a zombie.

The next day, I stopped at Fahy's Daybreak in Turloughmore and the lady at the deli counter said to me, 'Christ almighty, what happened you the other night? You weren't yourself.' I stopped at a petrol station in Portarlington a couple of days later and the cashier said to me, 'You weren't yourself on the *Late Late Show*. Were you alright?' Then that week I went to the Ploughing Championships and about twenty people stopped me over the two days with the same question. It was as if the whole country was my family and they copped that I wasn't 100 per cent. *Ní raibh mé istigh liom féin ar an Late Late.*

Sioctha
Numb/frozen

[shuk-ha]

Bhí an baile ar fad sioctha leis an nuacht an lá sin.
The whole town was numb from the news that day.

Only comes in winter time when the grass is crunchy, the water is frozen, and the heating is on full blast.

'*Sioctha*' comes from '*sioc*', the Irish for 'frost'. *Sioc* only comes in winter time when the grass is crunchy, the water is frozen, and the heating is on full blast. It epitomises that white, frosted landscape you see when you look out the window from your cosy house.

It's amazing how many phrases in Irish have grown out of words we use for nature. When you are numb, it is as if you are frozen in place from tragedy, so it's a poignant evolution of the word '*sioc*'. I would also use it to say someone was in shock, another emotional state born out of bad news. It's no doubt a sad word, but there's a stillness to '*sioctha*' that's beautifully descriptive.

Cráite
Heartbroken

[craw-tcha]

Tá mo chroí cráite leis an leaid seo.
That young lad has my heart broken.

A sad, sad word for when you don't even have any energy left to cry.

'Cráite' is a sad, sad word for when you don't even have any energy left to cry. It can be used for really bad break-ups, after you've been with someone for 10 years and you have to go about living separate lives from each other. It's the wailing mother waving her son off at the airport because he's emigrating to find a better way of life and she knows she won't see him again for a couple of years. *Cráite* is part and parcel of life in Ireland, from the emigration in the '80s to history repeating itself now. I'd say the people who work in departures in Knock and Shannon airports have seen their fair share of *cráite* parents over the years. It describes a high level of sadness. *Bhí a croí briste* (her heart was broken) is bad, but *bhí sí cráite* is worse. It is pure tragedy.

Faoi bhrú
Stressed/under pressure

[fwee vroo]

I rith na hArdteiste, bhí na mílte scoláirí timpeall na tíre faoi bhrú.
During the Leaving Cert, thousands of students around the country were stressed.

I checked for my passport.
Jeans, jacket, bag. No sign.
Stress starting.

I only get sort of stressed, not even full-on stressed, the odd time. Having said that, I was really under pressure there a few years ago when I lost my passport in Wales on a four-day stag.

On the Thursday we had a party in a stone cottage in the Welsh countryside. My mate Phil was blasting out the music, and we were all dancing to classic Carl Cox, decent tunes. It was full-on Stag Mode.

I woke up on the Monday in a small city-centre hotel in a daze and packed my bag, sick as a dog, head throbbing, and waited downstairs for the 16 other casualties to arrive. Then I checked for my passport. Jeans, jacket, bag. No sign. Stress starting.

I went back up to the room. Bed, wardrobe, locker. No sign. The lads are all ready, the flight back to Knock is soon, and East Midlands Airport is four hours away. Stress mounting.

We get to the car rental place and my mind is racing. It's gone. So I call Foreign Affairs in Ireland, and they say I'll have to go to London to get a replacement passport. I am *faoi bhrú anois*.

We hop into the rental car, and I say, 'Lads, can we go back to the house we stayed in on Thursday?' We check Google Maps and thankfully it's on the way to the airport. We pull up, the front door to the cottage is open, and I race into the sitting room. And there it is in a pile of CDs, sandwiched between Carl Cox and Leftfield. I've never been more elated to be catching a flight to Knock Airport.

Tá imní orm
I'm apprehensive

[taw im-nee ur-em]

Tá X-ray *agam ar maidin – tá imní orm faoi.*
I've an X-ray in the morning – I'm apprehensive about it.

When the coffee you stopped for at the Applegreen doesn't agree with you and you're on the way to Dublin for an interview.

This little four-letter word is bursting with the jitters. '*Imní*' is that feeling you get before your Leaving Cert exams, when the hormone of apprehension kicks in. It's for the occasions when the coffee you stopped for at the Applegreen doesn't agree with you and you're on the way to Dublin for an interview, or for when you have butterflies in your stomach before the county final. It's a small word for the big moments, or even the small moments that you have big feelings about, like asking someone out for the first time.

One of the biggest feelings of *imní* I can remember has to be my driving test. I don't think there's a person who doesn't feel apprehensive when the tester says, 'Open the bonnet there and show me where you put the water in.' There are so many things running through your head: do they look cross, is it going to rain, what the fuck is a demister? I didn't learn to drive until I was 28 and I did my test through Irish thinking I might get more points out of it, that maybe the tester would like the show on TG4. They didn't blink an eye when they called my name, but I did pass first time, so you never know.

Ar mhuin na muice
On the pig's back

[air mwin na mwi-ka]

Bhí muid ar mhuin na muice i ndiaidh don Mhí an ceann is fearr a fháil ar Bhaile Átha Cliath.
I was on the pig's back (delighted) after Meath beat Dublin.

One I use when I get great news about a friend.

We use 'on the pig's back' all the time in Ireland, and it's the literal translation of the Irish *'ar mhuin na muice'*. We were the first great pig-riders of Europe. I don't know whether the Irish or English came first, or why being on a pig's back would make you happy, but I do know the expression is hundreds of years old. It's one I use when I get great news about a friend. They got a job in Seattle or passed their exams or got a place on the county football team. It's a way of celebrating success, because they're all set up now, away in a hack.

It builds on the Holy Trinity of inner contentment (page 97), yet another way to express happiness in Irish. But we tend to use this phrase more about other people than about ourselves, which is lovely in itself. We're happy for people who are on the pig's back, the little moments like when someone has bought their first car or got a promotion at work. It's about us celebrating other people's good luck.

Meidhreach, súgach, ar meisce, caochta
Merry, tipsy, drunk, ossified

[my-rokh, soo-gakh, er meshka, kwee-okhta]

Thosaigh mé ag ól sa ghrian in Inis Mór, níorbh fhada go raibh mé meidhreach.
I started drinking in the sunshine in Inis Mór, wasn't long before I was merry.

When the craic is good in the local and everyone is having a few pints, and which word you choose depends on what roundabout you want to get off at.

Now we're on an adventure of drunkenness. The Dual Carriageway of Intoxication. *'Meidhreach'* happens after the first few kilometres, *'súgach'* after another few, *'ar meisce'* when you're well on your way, and *'caochta'* when you've forgotten where you were going in the first place. They're beautiful words for when the craic is good in the local and everyone is having a few pints, and which word you choose depends on what roundabout you want to get off at.

You've had a couple of pints and you might think you're a bit *meidhreach*, but then you have a little speed wobble on your way to the jacks and you realise you're actually fairly *súgach*.

A lot of people might already be familiar with *'ar meisce'*, which just means 'drunk', but *'caochta'* is an advanced Irish word for an advanced level of drunkenness. Someone who is *caochta* is utterly ossified. You might have a flush in your cheeks, and then you're giddy so you stop caring where you're supposed to be or what's for dinner, but if you get *caochta*, you've left the road to merriment and you're on your way to Narnia.

All of these Irish words have come to us from a time when there were thousands of distilleries in Ireland and we were making our own *poitín*. These words are for 'down at the crossroads and dance until morning' drinking, an inheritance of merriment passed down from our tribal ancestors.

Duine lách/duine fíorlách
Sound/super-sound person

[dinna lawkh/dinna feer-lawkh]

Duine lách é Sean Boylan, iar-bhainisteoir Cho. na Mí.
Seán Boylan the ex-Meath manager is a sound man.

> *You can use it for someone who might qualify in your mind as an 'absolute gent'.*

One of my favourite ways to describe people is 'sound'; I use it every day. *'Duine lách'* is the Irish equivalent. You can use it for someone who might qualify in your mind as an 'absolute gent'. They're the type of person who when they say to you, 'Will you do something for me?', you will do it, no bother at all. There's an energy about them, and you just want to pay respect to their soundness, because you know they'd go out of their way for you as well. It feels karmic.

'Duine lách' is a sound person and *'duine fíorlách'* is a super-sound person. It goes that extra mile to describe a legend. Everybody needs some sound friends in their lives. I'd love it if you'd take a step back from the book for a second and go, 'I know exactly who he's talking about.' It is the ultimate Irish compliment. I want to be a sound dad, a sound husband, a sound friend, and a sound coach, because if I'm sound, I know I'm a good person, so maybe somebody down the line will say, 'Hector, *is duine lách thú.*'

Fonn múisce
Gagging/nauseated/sickened

[fun moosh-ka]

Fuair me burgar ag an Great Wall of China *na blianta ó shin. Íosa Chríost, bhí fonn múisce orm ar feadh dhá lá ina dhiaidh.*
I got a burger years ago at the Great Wall of China. Jesus Christ, I was gagging for two days after it.

That 60-second warning you get in your stomach.

'*Múisc*' is the noun 'puke' in Irish. It's a visceral word, and I've even heard people use it as an adjective. That meal was puke. That movie was puke. That wedding dress was puke. Commentator Pat Spillane described the All-Ireland semi-final in 2003 as 'puke football' live on RTÉ. But you never want to bring *múisc* inside the doors of your house because it spreads like wildfire. You might try to be polite and say you had a 'tummy bug' or a 'bout of gastroenteritis', but we all know it was just a puking bug and it was carnage.

'*Fonn múisce*' is the cousin of '*múisc*'. It's that 60-second warning you get in your stomach. You feel as if it comes from the top of your brain all the way down through your body, and then you're running to the toilet – that gagging sensation you get before the main event. The word '*fonn*' means 'air', like a tune, so to have '*fonn múisce*' is to have an air of nausea come over you. It's a phrase you use for when someone or something is so awful that it makes you feel sick.

FOUR

Words from Gaeltacht days

I was sent to the Gaeltacht in Ráth Chairn when I was eight years old. Most parents these days probably wouldn't be sending their child off to speak Irish in a stranger's house at that age, but this was the '70s, and if I hadn't gone, I wouldn't be where I am now.

Before I went to the Gaeltacht, I didn't know there was another language. I didn't know you could laugh through Irish. I didn't think the food would taste the same through Irish. But you could, and it did. And in some ways, it was even better.

I immersed myself, and when the next summer came around, I said to Mam, 'I'd love to go back.' *'Ba bhreá liom dul ar ais.'* And that was it. By the time I was a teenager I'd already been going for four years, and I graduated to Big College – where the Irish was more advanced and so were my hormones. I *really* had to learn to communicate clearly if I was going to get the shift.

Ráth Chairn sparked my love of the language. It's a special place, lying deep in the fertile, green pasturelands of Co. Meath. The mad thing is, I was born and reared 12 miles from Ráth Chairn; I was blessed that my gateway to the language was just over the road. The first conversational words I learned were given to me by the people of the Ráth Chairn Gaeltacht when I was eight. I knew that I had to include the unusual, colloquial words from the area I picked up over the years to honour that gift. These words gave my Irish a richness and fluency that I want to pass on so you can enjoy using them as much as I do, because I wouldn't have any Irish inside me if it wasn't for Ráth Chairn.

An ndéanfaidh tú rince liom?
Would you like to dance with me?

[on nyayn-hee tu ring-ka lum]

Dia duit?
Dia is Muire duit.
Cád is ainm duit?
Is mise Síofra.
Is mise Hector, an ndéanfaidh tú rince liom, le do thoil?
Déanfaidh agus fáilte.
Hello.
Hello.
What's your name?
I'm Síofra.
I'm Hector, would you like to dance with me please?
I'd be delighted.

> *This phrase was vital if you wanted to be able to confidently ask a girl to dance with you.*

Those early céilís were formative. Over the first week or so you could lay the groundwork so possible relationships could blossom. Learning this phrase was vital if you wanted to be able to confidently ask a girl to dance with you. '*An ndéanfaidh tú rince liom?*' I can almost hear my young Navan voice saying it. There was a girl from Trim, another one from Dunboyne, the Walls of Limerick with a girl from Limerick. You ask the question, she says 'Yes', and then there's the holding of hands. CONTACT!

You never forget the Gaeltacht romances, especially that night back at the house and the craic in your *seomra*, lying on bunk beds chatting with the boys about the girls. 'Lads,' I'd say, 'I'm going to ask her to go out with me.' Then it's another piece of grammar to master.

An rachaidh tú amach liom?
Will you go out with me?

[awn rocky too ah-mok lum]

A Shíofra, an rachaidh tú amach liom?
Ní rachaidh mé amach leat.
Cén fáth?
Mar is maith liom buachaill eile.
Síofra, will you go out with me?
No, I won't go out with you.
Why?
Because I like another boy.

After all the glancing and smiling and dancing, it comes down to this moment.

The most important question of the whole three weeks in the Gaeltacht. You've been building up to it for days. After all the glancing and smiling and dancing, it comes down to this moment. You have enough of the language, you know the verb, you have the future tense: *rachaidh mé ann amárach* (I will go there tomorrow). So you're almost there: all you have to do is turn the future tense into a question and then it's game on.

It's the last dance of the night, and if all goes well, you'll gain entry to '*Grúpa* Nookie Club' – those five minutes at the end of the night when 'couples' can shift the head off each other, or at least attempt to, in the corner of the hall.

I fancied this girl one year, and in my head I'd made all the right moves, sent out all the right signals, and so I asked her, '*An rachaidh tú amach liom?*' There was a pause. '*Cén fáth?*' she says. Why? WHY? I was goosed, gobsmacked; I wasn't expecting that response. '*Eh ... ehmmm ... Mar is maith liom thú?*' Because I like you? Another pause, then finally, '*Ceart go leor.*' Phew! And off we headed to the *Grúpa* Nookie Club corner. It's no wonder I was begging to go back to the Gaeltacht for two full months at the age of 14.

Gadhar
dog

[guy-er]

Tá gadhar agam.

I have a dog.

> *I love using it when I see a scruffy, wild-looking dog.*

No offence to the word *'madra'*, but *'gadhar'* sounds even more Irish. It's a gorgeous word I learned as a young lad in Ráth Chairn, where they only say *'gadhar'* and never say *'madra'*. For me, I love using it when I see a scruffy, wild-looking dog. It's a word that fills my mind with images of a *hound*: a big aul dog that isn't going to look in the kitchen window at you with sad eyes when a drop of rain falls. It's a busy working dog, out in the fields all day and patrolling the back yard at night. You wouldn't catch a *gadhar* jumping up on the sofa to watch *Gogglebox* or going off to Mutts 'n' Cuts for a pedicure and a blow dry. No chance. I couldn't imagine Cú Chulainn standing on the Hill of Tara with his *madra* beside him, but Cú Chulainn and his *gadhar*? Now you're talking!

Ag déanamh láichín
Rubbing/stroking gently

[egg day-niv lawk-een]

Déan láichín leis an madra, tá sé cúthaileach.
Pet the dog there gently, he's shy.

> *The kind of gentle rub that pulls back their eyebrows and flattens their ears, and them smiling up at you like a maniac.*

As long as I can remember, we have always had Jack Russells in the family. My first dog was called Brandy. He was a great little dog, proud and quick. He starred in the Christmas play in my primary school in Navan when fifth and sixth class presented *The Wizard of Oz*. They needed a dog to play the role of Toto, Dorothy's trusted friend, and Brandy got the part. He stole the show and got five-star reviews in the *Meath Chronicle* for his performance on the Yellow Brick Road (in Navan you've made it if you're in the *Meath Chronicle*).

Now we have a Jack Russell called Rocco, and there's nothing more pleasant and rewarding than petting his head. A long stroke that starts at the snout, goes over the head and down the back of the neck. The kind of gentle rub that pulls back their eyebrows and flattens their ears, and them smiling up at you like a maniac. There's a thing that Rocco does all the time when I drive up in the car, arriving home: he shows his teeth. It looks weird, but he's smiling. Apparently it's a thing that Jack Russells do. A big, wide grin showing all his teeth because Daddy's home. It's class. Even before I'm out of the car, he's up at the door to welcome me, and I greet him with a big rub on the head, *ag déanamh láichín le* Rocco, both so happy to see each other.

Laoidín/lao beag óg
Small baby calf

[lee-deen / lee byug owg]

Tá an laoidín sin dubh agus bán.
That small calf is black and white.

> We had a small field at the back of the house with a little shed where there was always a cow in calf.

We all have memories from childhood ingrained deep in our minds. Mine are about growing up in the countryside. We had a small field at the back of the house with a little shed, and there was always a cow in calf. My favourite cow was named Blue because of her grey-blue colour, and she was in calf most years. One January, in the middle of a hard midlands frost, I woke up to my father's voice: 'Get up. The cow's calfing. I need a hand.'

It was freezing. The land was white and crispy, steam rising from the heat of Blue in labour as she slowly pushed the calf out. Suddenly my father shouted at me to get a rope from the garage. I ran out but couldn't find it, and he was shouting, 'Hurry up, hurry up', so under pressure I grabbed a skipping rope. I rushed back and Dad tied the skipping rope around the calf's legs and said, 'OK, hold that and pull nice and slow.' With a little effort the calf arrived safely onto the frozen grass. My father showed me how to clear its airway and nostrils and that was it, a new arrival at the Ó hEochagáins'. We put the afterbirth close to the hedge for the local fox and left Blue with her *lao beag óg*. I was shattered. It was 4 a.m., I was 12 years old, and I'd just helped deliver my first calf. A couple of hours later I was walking into school as a first year, and I had maths first class.

Garraithe/garrantaí
Fields/paddocks

[gaaw-ree/gawr-an-tee]

Tá na beithígh sna garrantaí.
The cows are in the fields.

There was a view of a field from every window in our house in Knockumber.

There's something about '*garraí*' as opposed to '*páirc*' that shows the importance of fields to the people of Ireland, whether they're working fields in rural areas or playing fields in cities.

I was born in a house in the middle of fields. We lived only two miles from the town, but it was pure countryside. There was a view of a field from every window in our house in Knockumber – the fields where we played, the fields that we used as shortcuts – and we knew who owned each field and where they lived. I knew which field was on the far side of every hedge and ditch. The fields smelled different through the seasons. They looked different, too: tall grass and summer meadows, buttercups and dandelions, dry ground and wet soil. I knew which one had the nettles and, most important, where to go in the field to get the cure of a dock leaf after a good stinging.

My father taught me many things, including how to wipe my arse with a dock leaf if I was far from the house and nature called. 'It's as good as any toilet paper,' he'd say. And I'll tell you what, it did the job. He also taught me where to find mushrooms, when to look for them, and how to cook them. The best time to pick them was when the cattle had done their grazing, left fresh cow pats, the sun had warmed the land up for a day or two, followed by a soft fall of rain. Then there they would be, hidden away in clumps of grass: the freshest, most delicious mushrooms that seemed to pop up overnight.

Now where my house once was surrounded by *garraithe* full of mushrooms and dock leaves, there's a TK Maxx and a Burger King.

Brádán báistí
Drizzle

[braw-dawn bawsh-tee]

Tá sé ag báisteach taobh amuigh ach níl ann ach brádán.
It is raining outside but it is only a drizzle.

The drizzle that starts in the west at the Galway Arts Festival in July and doesn't stop until the following May.

No other nation in the world knows rain like Ireland. All conversation is shushed in the sitting rooms of the country at 9.30 p.m. every night, and we wait in silence to hear the weather. After the four-day forecast and the '80s-style graphics, the conversation resumes: 'Jesus, it's given bad for Wednesday and Thursday.' 'Christ! Look at the rain that's promised.' Then we head to our beds, happy we know the weather.

But no matter the occasion, there'll always be some sort of rain. The Galway Races? Rain. The Ploughing? Lashing rain. The wedding photos outside the church? Torrential. And in between the heavy rain we have the drizzle that starts in the west at the Galway Arts Festival in July and doesn't stop until the following May. Drizzly aul drizzle day in, day out. *Brádán báistí* is a phrase my mate Alan O'Reilly of the 'Carlow Weather' X account should know. He's the nation's weather guru and he would love a bit of *brádán báistí* descending over Mount Leinster in the distance from his back garden.

Ag gleadhradh báistí
Pelting rain/lashing rain

[egg gler-ra bawsh-tee]

Tá sé ag gleadhradh báistí an tráthnóna ar fad.
It is lashing rain all afternoon.

> *You're at the pitch, the wipers are on full blast, you're trying to keep the windscreen from fogging up and the rain is so bad you can't get out of your car.*

You're at the pitch, the wipers are on full blast, you're trying to keep the windscreen from fogging up, and the rain is so bad you can't get out of your car. But your seven-year-old is absolutely soaked to the skin in an under-8s challenge, and he hasn't even touched the ball yet. So you get out to tell him you're there as he leaves the pitch drenched, sopping, cold and shaking.

Now, the key to all those weekends standing on the sidelines while it's *ag gleadhradh báistí* is a good golf umbrella. I have three in the boot at all times. One for my head, one for my legs, and one for the other parents to huddle under because they didn't come prepared. One of the brollies is from the local farm-agri store near me, a weapon of an umbrella. This yoke could stand up against gale-force winds and sideways rain. I've been coaching for the last 10 years at my local club, Claregalway, and to be in the dressing room after a victory in the lashing rain is one of the greatest places to be. The steam rising off the jerseys, spirits high, the pelting rain forgotten. Would you be anywhere else?

Meirbh marbhánta
Dead heat

[mer-iv mar-vawn-ta]

Tá sé meirbh marbhánta.
It is a dead heat.

> *The calmness of the air, when a sheet over you at night is too much and all the fans in the country have sold out in 24 hours.*

Heat rising off the road, ripples on the tarmac, the car a sweatbox – it's a warm summer's day when even the midges are trying to get suntans. *'Meirbh marbhánta'* really describes the 'dead' part of 'dead heat'. It's about the calmness of the air, when a sheet over you at night is too much and all the fans in the country have sold out in 24 hours. It even has pyjama-wearers sprawled on their beds in the nip with the windows flung open hoping for a whisper of a breeze.

It's the type of weather you usually only get on a foreign holiday, all slathered in aftersun heading out for dinner. I've felt it on my travels in Cuba, and I've felt it in Navan during the Leaving Cert of 1986. The World Cup was on in Mexico and we felt like we were there ourselves, playing football till all hours with the sweat pouring off us, celebrating goals like we were the Maradonas of Meath. What used to be a shock to the system is now a frequent feature of summers in Ireland, with plenty of opportunities to complain about the heat and say, '*Tá sé meirbh marbhánta.*'

Ceapann sé gurb é féin a rug é féin
A cocky person

[cyap-in shay gur-rib ay hain a rug ay hain]

Tá an leaid sin chomh bainte amach, ceapann sé gurb é féin a rug é féin!
Yer man is so full of himself, he thinks he gave birth to himself.

*There's one in every parish,
every team and every boardroom.*

This is a poetic and precise way to describe someone as cocky. It literally translates as 'he thinks he gave birth to himself'. It's cutting, that's for sure. Irish has some of the most beautiful ways to describe things, even when you're insulting someone.

We've all met someone like this: there's one in every parish, every team and every boardroom. They're usually busy listening to themselves talk and doling out the 'Well, actuallys' in meetings. It's also a great description for the high-vis brigade. It's as if putting on a high-vis jacket gives them the power to be a gobshite, like they're Joseph and the Amazing Technicolor Dreamcoat but it's just Finbar and his clipboard at the local AGM.

You would have to be some height of cocky to think you gave birth to yourself, so use this one wisely.

Bainte amach
Full of himself

[bwin-tcha amok]

Tá an leaid sin Liam Gallagher chomh bainte amach.
That lad Liam Gallagher is full of himself.

The type of swagger that Liam Gallagher from Oasis or Ian Brown from the Stone Roses have when they walk out on stage.

We love having 101 ways to say the same thing in Ireland, so here's another phrase for 'cocky', although it's more about being confident than arrogant. *'Bainte amach'* is the type of swagger that Liam Gallagher from Oasis or Ian Brown from the Stone Roses have when they walk out on stage, or the likes of David Clifford from Kerry when he's out on the pitch. I think we should all try to have a bit of swagger about us. It's hard to find it, and it takes time to get, but once you have it, keep it. It's a phrase for the people who can really show what they can do when they're performing, whether it's sport or music or acting.

It took me years to work up to having confidence, but the Gaeltacht was like my Billie Barry school of performance. I learned the skills to talk to people, to not feel nervous in front of a crowd, and to be confident in my own ability and my appearance. By the time I was a *cúntóir* at 15 or 16 years of age, I could stand up in front of one hundred teenagers and teach them a song or dance. It's the *'bainte amach'* I developed there from being able to make people laugh that gave me the confidence to audition for the show on TG4. There's a thin line between showing off and having a bit of swagger, but I don't think being *'bainte amach'* is always a bad thing.

Chomh milis le mil
Fake person

[ko mill-ish le mill]

An bhean sin, tá sí chomh milis le mil.
Yer woman there, she is as fake as anything.

They love stupid office talk like 'vis-à-vis' and 'let's circle back at close of business'.

This is one for the David Brent types who throw their weight around in work. They come into the meeting all 'Good morning. How are you?' but you know you can't trust the big, sweet grin on their face. They love stupid office talk like *'vis-à-vis'* and 'let's circle back at close of business' but there's no substance behind it. The phrase translates more literally as 'sweet as honey', but it's so sweet it will make you sick. Your friend might be *'chomh milis le mil'* when they come over to see your new kitchen and they say, 'It's very you,' but you know they really mean, 'I think it's horrible.' It's a great phrase to describe politicians when they're trying to get your vote, but you know they won't do half the things they're promising. 'He said he's going to solve the housing crisis and cut my taxes. *Tá sé chomh milis le mil.*'

Tuilleadh diabhail agat
Good enough for ya

[tchilla jowl att]

A Dhaid, tá slaghdán orm.
Nach ndúirt mé leat seaicéad a chaitheamh oíche
Dé Sathairn?
Rinne mé dearmad.
Tuilleadh diabhail agat. Now, *amach as an leaba.*
Dad, I've a cold.
Didn't I tell you to wear a jacket on Saturday night?
I forgot.
Good enough for you. Now, get out of that bed.

> *You hear it from your mother when you're a teenager and she tells you to put on a jacket but you don't, so you come home shivering and sopping wet.*

This phrase is for the 'I told you so' moments. It's not a bad thing, but it's passive-aggressive. You hear it from your mother when you're a teenager and she tells you to put on a jacket but you don't, so you come home shivering and sopping wet. *'Bhuel, tuilleadh diabhail agat!'* I could do an awful lot of things as a dad when my boys were younger, but I couldn't get a 10-year-old to wear a jacket to school. Now that they're teenagers it's gum shields: 'What do you mean you can't find your gum shield? Didn't I tell you to put it in your bag?'

It's a handy one for any domestic mishap and I hear it at home regularly myself. I'd say I have 25 pairs of those white, flimsy hotel slippers. I'm a serial slipper-stealer. They're meant for lush carpets and small mileage, trips to the hotel door when the room service arrives. But I take them home and wear them out the back in the middle of winter. And when I slip in the rain and my arse hits the doorstep, I hear a clear *'Tuilleadh diabhail agat'* from my wife.

Le haghaidh
Pregnant

[leh hi-g]

Tá Máire le haghaidh.
Máire is expecting.

Has a feeling of the future about it, that you're waiting in anticipation for the arrival of a baby.

'*Le haghaidh*' is a beautiful way of saying 'pregnant' and it's colloquial to Ráth Chairn. I've never heard it anywhere else, and it's one of the newer phrases in my Irish vocabulary, but it's one I'll be using all the time now that I know it. It means 'expecting' and it's much nicer than '*torrach*', which is the word we commonly use in Irish to say 'pregnant'. You just know someone wearing a white shirt in the Department of Education came up with '*torrach*' in the 1950s. It sounds clinical, as if being '*torrach*' is something you wouldn't really be telling anyone. In English you might say, 'She fell pregnant,' which makes it sound like gossip. But '*le haghaidh*' is beautiful. It has a feeling of the future about it, that you're waiting in anticipation for the arrival of a baby. It's to be looked forward to.

Lámhacán
Crawling

[law-va-con]

Bhí sup maith agam aréir. Bhí mé ag lámhacán isteach go dtí an leaba ag a trí a chlog ar maidin.
I had a good sup last night. I crawled into bed at three o'clock in the morning.

> *When a child starts to move and all of a sudden, they're creeping from the kitchen to the hallway to the bottom of the stairs.*

'*Lámhacán*' means 'to be using the hands' or 'to be handy'. The '*acán*' at the end of '*lámh*' is used in loads of places in Irish. You can tack it on to the end of a word to make it mean 'the place of that thing', so '*seomra glanacháin*' is a 'cleaning room' or '*meaisín níocháin*' is 'the machine of the washing'.

'*Lámhacán*', though, is when a child starts to move and all of a sudden they're creeping from the kitchen to the hallway to the bottom of the stairs. I remember fitting the stair gates in my house to stop my two baby boys from attempting the perilous climb up the stairs. We had one at the bottom and one at the top, and of course I left them up long after the crawling stopped. I think they were teenagers by the time I took them down, practically able to jump over the gates. The contraptions were hard enough to open at the best of times, but trying to get through them quietly after I'd returned from the local with a good sup on board was near impossible. I'd be locked and '*ag lámhacán*' into bed at three o'clock in the morning.

Fuarchaoineadh
Sobbing

[fur-kwee-na]

Stop an fuarchaoineadh anois, níl tada ort.
Stop that sobbing now, there is nothing wrong with you.

The dark art of crying but not really crying, the tears that go nought to sixty in a split second.

Parents of small children know this type of crying well. It's the dark art of crying but not really crying, the tears that go nought to sixty in a split second and can be turned off just as quick. It is Hollywood-level crying, when your child has a meltdown because you won't buy Wagon Wheels in the supermarket. They go into a full-tilt crying fit … and they switch it off the second you put the Wagon Wheels in the trolley. It's the kind of crying that inevitably kicks off at mass, at the school gates, anywhere public to get maximum manipulation.

A lot of people will know the word *'caoineadh'* for 'crying', but *'fuarchaoineadh'* expresses that extra level of drama. It's also a phrase that might be useful for 'man flu' crying, when you're lying on the couch feeling sorry for yourself with two tissues stuck up your nostrils and no one in the house gives a shit about you.

Tite i bhfeoil
They've put on weight

[tih-tcha ee vyohl]

Tá sé tite i bhfeoil.
He's after putting on a bit of weight.

> *You can almost imagine someone falling into a plate of roast beef when you hear it.*

The word *'feoil'* in Irish means 'meat', so the literal translation of this phrase is 'he's fallen into meat'. It's another one I picked up from the people of Ráth Chairn that paints a picture so beautifully. You can almost imagine someone falling into a plate of roast beef when you hear it. There's nothing malicious in it either. It's how most of us feel after Christmas or a good holiday. We seem to love talking about weight in Ireland and we almost greet each other with 'How are you? You've lost a bit of weight.' But saying someone has 'put on weight' is so literal, and I don't know of a similar phrase in English that gives so much detail in just three words.

Phrases like *'tite i bhfeoil'* that have been passed down generations of native Irish-speakers are pure poetry. I'm still learning the language, picking up new words every day, and when I come across phrases like this, it sets my brain fizzing.

FIVE

On Inis Meáin time

If Ráth Chairn was my Irish college, I got my PhD on Inis Meáin. It was my time on the island that really put the polish, or the *snas*, on my Irish. I had gone to Trinity College Dublin at 17 to do a degree in Early and Modern Irish, decided not to turn up to my classes, and swiftly failed out. So me and a few friends decided to take ourselves to Inis Meáin for a while, and I ended up staying for two years.

I lived in a little house called Sunsplash Cottage. I had the back bedroom, and straight out my window there was a very fine stone wall, and another fine stone wall behind it, and more stone walls behind that. But out the window of the sitting room I could see Inis Oírr and the tower on the Cliffs of Moher.

I'll never forget the day I stepped off the *Rose of Aran* at the pier and I heard the Irish of Inis Meáin for the first time. It was the most beautiful, deep, mysterious Atlantic Irish, and my God did they speak it at 100 miles an hour. It was the University of Inis Meáin, and it gave me the keys to the language, without a shadow of a doubt. I knew I had graduated when I was able to stop on the road and have a chat with the locals. And by the time I was leaving to move back to the mainland, I'd been given the gift of the islanders' discount on the boat as well.

A lot of the words I learned there are very much a reflection of the environment. They're beautiful, descriptive words that you're unlikely to hear anywhere else. But if you find yourself on the island and you throw a few of these into conversation, you'll be warmly welcomed.

Lig do scíth
Take a rest

[lig duh shkee]

Suigh síos ansin cois tine agus lig do scíth.
Sit down there by the fire and take a rest.

*A lovely bit of time to relax,
to chill, to take a break.*

I had to learn how to *'lig mo scíth'* properly on Inis Meáin. It took me the best part of a year to get used to the pace of life on the island. The sun rises and the sun sets, the Sunday papers come in on a Tuesday, and what happens in between happens on island time.

You could measure time on the island by the sound of the plane arriving (eleven o'clock), the hum of the boat engine as it pulled into harbour (two o'clock), and the sound of it leaving again (four o'clock). There was no need for a watch when you had your ears, because there were few other sounds on the island.

When I first arrived, I didn't know how to deal with it. I'd go to the shop to find it closed with no clue when it would open again. But after a while, I began to see these in-between moments as a gift. It's a lovely bit of time to relax, to chill, to take a break. *Lig do scíth.* Take in the freshest of fresh sea air, the sound of water and waves all around, and when it's warm and the sun is shining and the sea is calm, there's nothing more beautiful than sitting down on a flat rock and taking five.

Carcair
Hill

[cor-ker]

Níos faide thuas an carcair tá Dún Conchúir.
Further up the hill you have Conor's Fort.

Not a cnoc like Diamond Hill or
a sliabh like Carrauntoohil,
but will still take the wind out of you.

Hills on the Aran Islands are pretty common. There's a lot of ups and downs, twists and turns, and rises on the roads that don't look steep, but when you walk them, you know all about it. The houses of Inis Meáin were all built on the eastern side of the island, house after house cut into the stone hills, safe from the wild ferocity of wind and water that can hit the place.

A *carcair* is a specific type of hill. It's not a *cnoc* (hill) like Diamond Hill or a *sliabh* (mountain) like Carrauntoohil, but a *carcair* will still take the wind out of you. I liked to walk up one of Inis Meáin's hills at night when the lights of the houses illuminated the island like a jewel, and I'd sit up there at the top and gaze across the whole of Galway Bay, from Connemara to An Spidéal to the lights of Galway City. Stone and rock are in the DNA of the islanders: they've adapted to it, they've reared families on it, and they've farmed it. It's no wonder they have their own unique word for the stony hills you find dotted around the land.

Scallóg fuisce
A shot or 'nip' of whiskey

[skaw-lowg fwish-ka]

Caith amach scallóg fuisce dom ansin agus pionta.
Throw me out a shot of whiskey and a pint.

He would have his pint and a scallóg *of Powers every day at the same time.*

After I'd spent five or six months living on the island, the locals started to get to know me. Everyone knows everybody and news travels fairly quickly on any small island when new people move in, but it took a while for them to take to me. The key was when I could hold a conversation in Irish when out and about, like an islander stopping on the road to have a chat about the weather.

The only pub on Inis Meáin was bang in the heart of the island: a long, white-washed stone cottage with a thatched roof. It would open around midday for the regulars, maybe two or three older men. Real island men, fishermen or farmers who had done whatever needed to be done in the morning and would stroll down for an afternoon pint. It was a low-lit pub, but as you entered the sun would shine through the door, and you'd see the long, lounge-type seats against the walls. The regulars would sit down quickly in their usual spots, from where they could monitor the bar and the people who came in off the boat.

I became friendly with a fisherman called Ruairí Beag Ó Flatharta. He would have his pint and a *scallóg* of Powers every day at the same time. I was honoured the first day I ever sat with him and chatted. He was a lovely soft man who had stories upon stories. We enjoyed each other's company, and we would sit beside each other, our backs to the wall, sometimes in silence. Ruairí taught me to slow down to the pace and rhythm of the island and enjoy a pint of stout and a *scallóg fuisce* in the afternoon sun.

Scata
A crowd (of people)

[skah-ta]

Bhí scata maith daoine ann.
There was a good crowd of people there.

The pinnacle of compliments for any event.

'*Scata*' is a lovely way of saying there was a good crowd at something. We adore good turnouts at functions, whether it's a coffee morning or a senior semi-final. And we are great at providing a good *scata* to support a local sponsored anything: sponsored haircut, sponsored walk, George and Mary doing the tango at the Strictly Come Damhsa fundraiser in the community centre. It's the pinnacle of compliments for any event.

'How was the funeral?'
'Aaah, it was very sad but there was a great turnout.'

The population on Inis Meáin isn't huge, but there were a few times on the island where I encountered a *scata*, the most memorable of them being when the door of the pub was locked and we had a real late one. '*Bhí scata maith ann ag a trí a chlog ar maidin.*' 'There was a good crowd there till three o'clock in the morning.'

Slócht
Hoarseness

[shlowkt]

Tá slócht orm i ndiaidh an scréachaíl ar fad ag an gcluiche.
I am hoarse after all the shouting at the game.

That deep, gravelly hoarseness you have after three days in Cheltenham.

I'd never heard the Irish word for 'hoarse' till I landed in Inis Meáin. That's why I loved the place. My Irish was flourishing. The rhythm, the tones, the style or *'blas'*, as it's called. The Connemara speed of delivery and turns of phrase. *'Slócht'* is a firm one now in my vocabulary. It's that deep, gravelly hoarseness you have after three days in Cheltenham screaming at horses like Dunguib and Annie Power. It's pure hangover voice, and definitely not to be confused with the *'sliocht'* you might hear at mass, when the priest says, *'Sliocht as an Soiscéal'*, 'A reading from the Gospel of ...' The pronunciation might be similar, but the meaning is *very* different.

Gread leat
Clear off

[grad lat]

Sin do dhótháin anois, gread leat!
That's enough out of you, clear off!

A phrase that you can bring out when the dog is crowding your ankles or when the wasps are trying to eat your ice cream in high summer.

This is a word I heard on the island to shoo away hens or a cat at your doorstep, or for gulls picking at your bins. I swear the seagulls in Ireland must be the biggest in the world. They're huge. They're getting fed, they're getting rent allowance, and they don't give a shit about you. I used to walk through Dublin City to Today FM when I filled in a few times for Ian Dempsey, and you'd want to see the seagulls around Grafton Street at six o'clock in the morning. Everyone's in bed and they're having their own seagull Electric Picnic. There I am shouting, *'Gread leat,'* trying to shoo them away so I can get to work, and the gulls are looking at me and saying in their best Dublin accents, 'You haven't a clue, pal. I run these fucking streets.'

'Gread leat' isn't usually used to refer to people, but it's a brilliant, fluent phrase that you can bring out when the dog is crowding your ankles or when the wasps are trying to eat your ice cream in high summer.

Ag gabháil fhoinn
Singing

[egg gow-all fyun]

Bhí muid ag gabháil fhoinn go dtí a sé a chlog ar maidin.
We were up singing till six in the morning.

> *For the beautiful* sean-nós *singing you might be lucky enough to hear in one of the great pubs in Connemara.*

If you did Irish in school, you might know *'ag canadh'* for 'singing', but I learned *'ag gabháil fhoinn'* a few miles across the sea in Inis Meáin. That's two different ways to say 'singing' in Irish, which shows you how important the tradition is in the Gaeltacht. It could be singing in the pub, in the kitchen, rocking a baby to sleep, or out on the currach pulling in the pots. If you can sing a song *as Gaeilge* in Inis Meáin or any public house in Connemara, you will be warmly received. I gave *'Peigín Leitir Móir'* a few verses in my time on the island, and it was always a crowd-pleaser.

But you wouldn't use *'ag gabhail fhoinn'* for just any type of singing. You wouldn't say in the residents' bar at three in the morning after a wedding, *'Ciúnas! Tá Dave ag gabháil fhoinn "American Pie".'* The phrase has ancient, tribal connotations, so you would use it for the beautiful *sean-nós* singing you might be lucky enough to hear in one of the great pubs in Connemara.

Scaití
Sometimes

[skaw-tee]

An ólann tú Bulmers?
Scaití sa samhradh b'fhéidir.
Do you drink Bulmers at all?
Ahh, the odd time in the summer maybe.

> *A word for something you might do two or three times a year, like going to mass for Christmas, christenings and weddings.*

'*Scaití*' is a lovely-sounding word and it's easy enough to pronounce. It means 'occasionally' or 'sometimes'. Even as a phrase, though, you would use it rarely, so you could say you only use '*scaití* ... *scaití*. It's a word for something you might do two or three times a year, like going to mass for Christmas, christenings and weddings.

> 'Do you still go to mass?'
> '*Scaití*. Mostly just at Christmas to keep the mammy happy.'
> 'Do you go to the gym?'
> '*Scaití*. But I still have me membership.'

I love these little words in Irish. 'The odd time' is nice in English, it does a good enough job, but '*scaití*' brings the idea of 'occasionally' to a higher level. When I say it, I can hear the whole of Connemara saying it. They've shared it with me, and now I'm passing it on to you. And don't be afraid to give it the full Connemara 'SKAW-tee'.

Aibéis
Ignorant

[aw-besh]

Is aibéis é.
He's an ignorant person.

The word they use on Inis Meáin to describe a complete ignoramus.

You can imagine what it's like on a small island with a population of less than two hundred people when you don't get on with someone. There would be no way to avoid them. To get by in such a small, remote location, it's all about harmony. You have to try and get on with each other, and everybody has to have the door open and a friendly spirit. Rifts and arguments will happen, though, so *'aibéis'* is the word they use on Inis Meáin to describe a complete ignoramus. Someone who is wilfully thick. The film *The Banshees of Inisherin* does a good job of showing some *aibéis* characters and what it's like to run into them day in, day out.

Sraoithil
Messy

[shri-hee-al]

Shiúil an fear isteach sa pub, seanleaid, agus cuma shraoithil air.
The man walked into the local pub, an oldish man, he looked dishevelled.

> *You mostly hear it on the island when people are talking about someone who is unkempt or wild-looking.*

'*Sraoithil*' can be used to describe a person or a thing, but you mostly hear it on the island when people are talking about someone who is unkempt or wild-looking in appearance. It's usually a person who doesn't look after themselves much. There were probably way more *daoine sraoithil* than there are now when this word came into being. Anyone *sraoithil* these days is likely trying to look that way on purpose, like Boris Johnson and his ruffled *gruaig*.

I like to use it to describe a messy room or house. There's a drawer in every kitchen in Ireland and it's called 'The Drawer of Shite Bits'. It contains everything but you can still find nothing. Its contents are a combination of birthday candles, old batteries, screws and washers, Banklink cards, keys you don't have doors for and 10 menus for a Chinese takeaway that closed down 15 years ago. To sum all of that up in one phrase, '*Íosa Críost, tá an drawer sin sraoithil!*'

Tá mé draoibéilte
I am destroyed

[taw may dree-bail-ta]

Sciorr mé sa bpuiteach agus bhí mo sheaicéid draoibéilte.
I slipped in the puddle of mud and my jacket was destroyed.

> *The cod hits the wall, the chips fly everywhere and there's curry sauce in one of the girls' hair. The place was destroyed and so was I.*

I guarantee you'll have occasion to use this word as soon as you put on your nice Christmas blouse or a crisp, white shirt. You will without a doubt spill gravy or red wine or both all over them. It's the law of the universe.

It happened me years ago in my tiny flat in Galway. There were about ten of us there on a Sunday evening, all hungover after partying all weekend, and we were going to watch a movie. So I got the kitty out and said I'd go to McDonagh's to get fish and chips, the best chipper in Galway.

I arrive back with 10 portions of fish and chips, and I'm like Gordon Ramsay with the garlic sauce and curry sauce and the vinegar. I put everything on plates and carry them into the living room one at a time to be careful, and everyone's happy because they're getting fed.

Now I'm dying for these fish and chips. They're swimming in vinegar and I can't wait to taste them. So of course I trip as I'm carrying my plate into the living room. The cod hits the wall, the chips fly everywhere, and there's curry sauce in one of the girls' hair. The place was destroyed and so was I. *Bhí mé draoibéilte.*

Scorach/fear mór ard
A big, tall man

[sku-rock]

Scorach é, is geall le fathach é.
He's a big tall man, like a giant.

> *Men who climbed majestically into the air in Croke Park, crashed and collided, then stood up again in an instant.*

We have been making big-framed, strong men in Ireland for thousands of years. The first big men I saw were the Men of Meath in the late '80s and early '90s. A squad of Giant Royal Warriors under the guidance of their leader, Seán Boylan. They were men who climbed majestically into the air in Croke Park, crashed and collided, then stood up again in an instant. Even the ads on TV in the '80s were full of big men holding up calves and dosing them with Panacur for the winter. Giants of GAA and giants of farming who were big enough to put a calf in a headlock and look like they were holding a kitten.

But the last time I saw a true *scorach* in the flesh, I was in SuperValu. A man stood beside me at the deli counter as I was buying ham and he was fucking gargantuan. I was so fascinated by his hugeness that I trailed him around the shop for a couple of aisles, marvelling at the broadness of his shoulders and the massiveness of his frame, and wondering how someone could produce such a beast of a man. I just wanted to know more about him: who he was and where his people came from. He was a *scorach* by all accounts, a mountain man of Ireland.

Tá rabharta ann
High tide

[taw rau-ar-ta aun]

Bhí rabharta mór ar farraige 's bhí na tonnta ag éirí ard.
There was a high tide and the waves were getting big.

Not just used to describe the 'tides' of water, it can also be used to describe a big movement or change in society.

There are four main high tides on Inis Meáin, and *'rabharta'* is the Irish word for the spring equinox or 'spring tide'. Everything on the island depended on what the sea was doing, whether the tide was in or out.

High tides have never been so relevant with the coastal flooding due to climate change, but I've included *'rabharta'* here because it's not just used to describe the 'tides' of water, it can also be used to describe a big movement or change in society. *'Rabharta mór glas'* means the 'big green wave', the push to fight for the environment against climate change. There's a lovely harmony to the word when you use it like that.

'Tá rabharta ann' is a phrase that all politicians should be aware of when they're throwing out the *cúpla focal* in interviews. It's when the people come together to form a *rabharta mór* that forces a big political or cultural shift. You see the tide in action when people gather to march and protest for a cause they believe in. It is the power of the sea used to describe the power of activism.

Tá bogadh sa bhfarraige
There's movement in the sea

[taw bug-a sa wah-rig-a]

Ní bheidh muid in ann snámh ansin inniu, tá bogadh sa bhfarraige.
We won't be able to swim today, there is movement in the sea/it is rough.

When the sea gets angry and it tells you, 'There's no messing today.'

This phrase is almost a warning. It wouldn't be used to describe the spray coming over the wall during your walk on Dún Laoghaire Pier. It's for when the sea gets angry and it tells you, 'There's no messing today.' So many phrases I learned on Inis Meáin relate to the sea. A lot of people on the island don't know how to swim, but they know the sea is to be respected. When you're 20 miles out in Galway Bay on a fishing boat and the next stop is America, you are well acquainted with the ferocious power of the Atlantic. Island people live and die by the sea. It has many characters and it can change in a split second. It can be your best friend one minute and your worst enemy the next.

The stretch of water between Inis Meáin and Inis Oírr is called *'An Sunda Salach'*, which means 'The Dirty Sound'. The name says it all – the roar and danger of the turbulent sea. If you use *'salach'* in Irish, it means dirty or treacherous. There are loads of these treacherous spots around the islands, and *'tá bogadh sa bhfarraige'* is an understated way of saying the sea is rough.

Tá an fharraige ina clár/
Tá an fharraige ciúin
The sea is calm

[taw an arr-ig-a inn-a klawr]

Níl gaoth ar bith ann, tá an fharraige ina clár.
There's not a pick of wind, the sea is calm.

*The sea is quiet, as flat as a board,
there isn't even a ripple.*

'*Clár*' in Irish means 'board', so '*clár dubh*' is 'blackboard'. This phrase uses '*clár*' to say the sea is quiet, as flat as a board, there isn't even a ripple. It has done its job for the day and now it's resting.

On a summer's evening on Inis Meáin, myself and the lads I lived with would head to the beach down from the house. It's hard to explain the balmy feeling of a summer's night on the island; the heat is different. The sky stretches on forever, a 360-degree canopy from the Burren to the Twelve Bens, and the glistening lights of Salthill and Galway way, way off in the distance. The beach we went to was called Trá Leictreach (Electric Beach). We would sit there and drink flagons of Linden Village that would arrive by plane – 12 flagons on a pallet ordered in from Roches Stores. The ghettoblaster would be booming the Stone Roses and the Happy Mondays. We would build stone statues from the rocks and after months they would look almost like miniature temples of stones dotted around the headland. Sitting there on a summer's night watching the islanders pull the evening lobster pots off shore, no wind, no waves, *bhí an fharraige ina clár*. The Atlantic Ocean between Inis Meáin and Inis Oírr seemed like it was relaxing, catching its breath. Sometimes we'd embrace the calmness and go in for a little dip, and there wasn't a dryrobe in sight.

Ronnach
Mackerel

[run-yokh]

Fuair mé píosa álainn ronnaigh don dinnéar.
I got a lovely bit of mackerel for dinner.

> *You could stick your hand in and come out with four or five mackerel.*

About a year into living on Inis Meáin, I got to experience mackerel season. There was a knock on the door just after 5 a.m. Up and out – it was going to be a busy morning. I got on the back of the Honda 50, two fishing rods in each hand, and we headed to the back of the island. Other Honda 50s and more rods would join us on the road. We were heading to a place called Coirnéal an Phráca, where straight across you could see Dún Aonghasa and the back of Inis Mór, and to the left the Cliffs of Moher and the far coast of north Kerry.

The rods were ready, the lines decorated with multicoloured feathers and hooks. One of the lads pointed out a seal bobbing in the water yards away from us, staring at us almost human-like. He said it was a signal. The seal was telling us that's they're here: *na ronnachaí*. It was time to catch some fish. From the first cast they were on the line, two and three fish at a time. I'd never seen anything like it.

Even I was catching some. You could stick your hand in and come out with four or five mackerel, there were that many. Then there would be mackerel to eat for weeks. Mackerel for breakfast, lunch and dinner. Boiled mackerel, fried mackerel, grilled mackerel. I'd open my freezer and there'd be 10 mackerel stuffed in beside the Crispy Pancakes. After about four weeks, I swore I'd never eat it again. But then the following September, the mackerel would be in again, and I'd be the first out with the rod.

Pabhsaer
Flower

[pow-sir]

Bhí na pabhsaeir amuigh in Inis Meáin.
The flowers were in full bloom on Inis Meáin.

A word used to describe the most beautiful island flowers that grow and thrive in these impossible conditions.

The locals of Inis Meáin use words that are found nowhere else on the island of Ireland. There's *'buaile'* for 'field', *'ceirtlín'* for 'ball of wool', and *'pluideog'* for 'nappy'. But one of the first words I learned while I lived there was their word for 'flower'.

It's a word I love to blow people's minds with when they ask about my time on Inis Meáin. 'Flower' is commonly known in Irish as *'bláth'*, but on Inis Meáin they say *'pabhsaer'*. On the island, there are flowers that pop up in the crevices of the expanses of flat rocks that stretch across the land, *'na creaga'* (the crags). The karst landscape is very similar to the Burren on the other side of the bay. *'Pabhsaer'* is a word used to describe the most beautiful island flowers that grow and thrive in these impossible conditions. The air is salty, fresh water is scarce, and all this flower needs is a tiny patch of soil to grow. The word blew me away, and when I learned it, I knew I was living in a very special place.

SIX

Words for romancing

'Romance' is a brilliant word. It conjures up images of movies and adventures and climbing out windows and taking selfies at the top of Diamond Hill. We need more of it in this country. It's the movements we do for weeks or months or years in a relationship, and then love starts living in the middle of it.

My romantic moments have always had destinations attached to them: a *céilí* with Dympna in Donegal, letters written to her from Inis Meáin, moving to the Basque Country together, and getting married in Rio de Janeiro. We've had splitting-the-rent romance and long-distance romance.

When I was on Inis Meáin, Dympna had a job in the Gaeltacht in Clare. She was boarding in an old convent building, and to get there I had to get the *Happy Hooker* boat from Inis Meáin to Doolin, then hitch all the way to Ennis, then get a lift off a friend to Carrigaholt. It was like *Planes, Trains and Automobiles*. I arrived late with nowhere to stay, and I wasn't supposed to be in the convent, but I really wanted to see her. So I climbed 40 feet up to her window at two o'clock in the morning. We spent a few hours together in her little room, and then I legged it down the fire escape at about six o'clock before we were caught. There's nothing like romance that involves a bit of danger and a long journey to get there. It was clear that I was *faoi gheasa aici* (page 230), and by then we had definitely reached *lánúin* status (page 216).

Spré
Dowry

[spray]

Bhí spré cheart réitithe ag an athair.
The father had a right good dowry ready.

You still hear people talking about wanting to marry someone who has their own house and a bit of road frontage.

Dowries are obviously a thing of the past, but you still hear people talking about wanting to marry someone who has their own house and a bit of road frontage. There was no shite-hawking about dowries in my marriage. I had no land, no car, no sheep, no property. Just a man from Meath and a woman from Clare. And we decided to do it our own way, so we eloped to Brazil to get married. There were only six people and a priest by the name of Fr John Cribbin from Shanagolden in Co. Limerick in the church in Rio de Janeiro. It was brilliant.

These days, dowries would probably include an air fryer, a gazebo and a set of rattan furniture. What I have is yours and what you have is mine, especially the Ninja juicer.

Lánúin
Couple

[law-noon]

Nach deas an lánúin iad!
Well aren't they a lovely couple!

> *When you've been together long enough to either be newly married or to have decided that living together is enough.*

It's practically the law in Ireland for a mammy to stop the car to have a gawk at a wedding and say, 'Ahhh, aren't they a lovely couple?' It's a term of endearment. By my estimation, there are four stages to a relationship, and being a *lánúin* is the third.

The first is 'they're going out', meaning they have left the house on multiple occasions to meet up.

The second is 'they're doing a line', one of the great phrases of the '70s and '80s, meaning they've been together for a little while.

Only then can you move on to the department of 'couples', the third stage, when you've been together long enough to either be newly married or to have decided that living together is enough.

The fourth stage is when you start mirroring each other's actions. This happens especially in the supermarket when you come out with two of everything.

> 'Did you get the Uncle Ben's sweet 'n' sour?'
> 'I did, yeah.'
> 'Oh, I did as well.'
> 'And did you get rice? Because I got rice.'
> 'I did, yeah.'

This is a phenomenon I like to call 'coupling up' rather than 'doubling up'. It's the synchronicity of long-term relationships when you can communicate without saying anything, but saying something would be helpful so you don't end up with two 24-roll packs of toilet paper.

Brídeog
Bride

[breed-ohg]

Ólfaimid sláinte na brídeoige!
Raise your glass to the bride!

Epitomises everything that the goddess stands for: strength, fearlessness, kindness and a big, massive cloak.

I always think of the Irish word *'brídeog'* breaking down as 'Bríd óg' or 'young Bríd', one of the most powerful warrior goddesses in Celtic mythology. So on behalf of all the women of Ireland, I've made the assumption that *'brídeog'* must come from the legend that was Bríd, and all *brídeog*s are Irish warrior princesses.

A *brídeog* epitomises everything that the goddess stands for: strength, fearlessness, kindness and a big massive cloak. *Brídeog*s should all have those long trains on their wedding dresses to pay respect to Bríd laying her cloak down in Kildare to claim the land. There are St Brigid's crosses being made in primary schools across Ireland that could be nestled into bouquets of flowers and thrown over the bride's shoulder at the end of the night, but they'd probably boomerang back and knock the head off a bridesmaid, such is their power.

My wife's middle name is Bridget so technically I married a Bríd. Having this association with the word *'brídeog'* is a way for all the Irish brides out there to connect to ancient Irish mythology and see themselves as goddesses on their big day.

Ag dul amach lena chéile
Going out with each other

[egg dull a-mock leh-na khay-la]

Táimid ag dul amach lena chéile.
We are going out with each other.

> *The deal clincher.*
> *It meant you could hold hands.*

It wasn't long after plucking up the courage to repeatedly ask someone to dance at the *céilí* each night at the Gaeltacht that you would ask them to go out with you. If they said yes, then you could say you were *'ag dul amach lena chéile'*. The deal clincher. It meant you could hold hands. You would meet up in the afternoons and play board games, which we called *cluichí beaga*, or if it was sunny you would go out on the field to play rounders, called *cluichí móra*. The whole relationship was blossoming throughout the day, and it all led up to the end of the *céilí* that night, at about nine o'clock, when you would kiss.

The relationship would be absolute bliss for about two days until you'd go off each other, and then it was right back to step one with someone else: *'An ndéanfaidh tú rince liom?'* 'Will you dance with me?' (page 142).

Staic
Good-looking man

[stack]

Nach breá an staic é!
He's a fine thing!

His dark curly hair and Atlantic-blue eyes, skin sallow from working outdoors, his broad shoulders casting a gorgeous shadow, biceps glistening in the evening sun.

I don't know how this word evolved but it packs a handsome punch. A *'staic'* is an Irish word for a fine-looking, strapping lad. There's never been a Mr Connemara contest to my knowledge, but there should be one televised live on TG4. There'd be *staicí* everywhere, and instead of doing a jig or reading a poem like the lovely girls in the Rose of Tralee, they would be emptying a trailer of turf, milking a cow, making a magnificent chowder, and telling you in under 60 seconds how much they love their mammies.

You can almost picture Mr Connemara in your mind. His dark curly hair and Atlantic-blue eyes, skin sallow from working outdoors, his broad shoulders casting a gorgeous shadow, biceps glistening in the evening sun as he pulls in the lobster pots. Then he spots you on the pier, turns his big frame towards you, looks you in the eye, and says ... *'Bhuel?'*

Stumpa
Good-looking woman

[stum-pa]

Nach breá an stumpa í!
Isn't she a fine-looking thing!

She can make you fall in love or cut you in two with a single turn of phrase.

It's a strong-sounding word, *'stumpa'*, which doesn't always make it sound like a compliment, but it is! You would hear it said in Connemara to describe a fine-looking lady, and there's plenty of them in Ireland. A *stumpa* can make you fall in love or cut you in two with a single turn of phrase. You can see her standing on the pier, eyes as green as seaweed, freckles decorating her nose, long curly hair blowing in the wind, with cheekbones like the MacGillycuddy's Reeks and something witty on the tip of her tongue.

It's like those scenes you see in *Game of Thrones* when a mysterious woman enters the castle, drops the hood of her cloak, and reveals the most beautiful face you've ever seen. Then the king turns to the knight and says, *'Nach breá an stumpa í?'*

I guarantee you the mysterious woman is played by Gráinne from Letterfrack as well, because there have been loads of Irish *stumpaí* through the ages:

Queen Maeve
The goddess Boann from Meath
Granuaile the Pirate Queen
Peig, the early years (NB, before she moved out to the island)
Any of the ladies who've ever presented the weather on TG4

Whether it's legacy *stumpaí* or modern-day *stumpaí*, *tá go leor stumpaí in Éirinn.*

An shiftáilfidh tú mé?
Will you shift me?

[on shift-all-ee too may]

An shiftáilfidh tú mo mhéit?
Will ya shift my friend?

I was the master of the shift when I was a teenager in the Gaeltacht.

I was the master of the shift when I was a teenager in the Gaeltacht. I had a great time during the summer and I was able to bring all that expertise back to my hometown in Navan and use it on the girls of Mercy Secondary School. I much preferred them to the Loreto girls because they were better kissers. So I became a Mercy girl aficionado. Some of my best teenage romances growing up were with them, so I want to give a big shout-out to any Mercy girls who might be reading this book!

By the time we were 17 or 18, me, my brother Freddy, and my friends were mad for the shift at the weekends. We used to go to Spider's, Diamond's, or the Hippodrome. Yes, there was a nightclub in Navan called the Hippodrome. It sounds like it should be in London or somewhere, but it was here in my hometown, and it had a split-level dance floor. This was the future of discos. It was pints, shift, pints, shift every weekend.

I don't know if 'shift' is still used by Irish teenagers these days, but you might still have luck with *'An shiftáilfidh tú mé?'* in the Gaeltacht.

Dualta i ngrá
Madly in love

[jool-ta i-ngraw]

Bhí mé dualta i ngrá léi chomh luath 's a leag mé súil uirthi.
I was madly in love from the first second I laid my eyes on her.

That summer love that takes over you when you're a teenager.

I have no disrespect for the words *'amore'* in Italian or *'amour'* in French, but there is no better word for love than *'grá'*. It's just a superior-sounding word, with the big, open 'AAAWW' at the end.

When I was a teenager, I fell madly in love two or three times every year in the Gaeltacht. It's that summer love that takes over you when you're a teenager. Courtown, Brittas Bay, Bundoran, Tramore are the most romantic destinations to a 16-year-old. They may as well be the Maldives.

If you fell in love as a teenager in Ireland in the '80s, it could only be for a week. But as I got older, I might fall madly in love only once every summer. To me now, being *dualta i ngrá* is that couple well into their seventies jiving at a family celebration, or the couple on the English *Gogglebox* who are always holding hands. I love watching older couples dancing together or walking arm in arm, because you can see they are *dualta i ngrá*. Madly in love.

Faoi gheasa aici
Under her spell/smitten

[fwee yassa ek-ee]

I bhfaiteadh na súl, bhí mé go hiomlán faoi gheasa aici.
In the blink of eye, I was under her spell (head over heels for her).

I couldn't take my eyes off her.

It was in a hotel called Óstán Ghleann Cholm Cille in Donegal on a November night in 1989 that I first laid eyes on Dympna. There was a traditional music session in the hotel and she was playing the tin whistle amongst her friends from Óg-Chlub na hInse, a youth club from Ennis. She had blonde hair and was wearing an orangey-gold blouse. I couldn't take my eyes off her.

It was the *Oireachtas*: a week-long celebration of Irish-speakers, musicians, and scholars alike. I plucked up the courage to ask her did she want a drink, *as Gaeilge* of course.

'Ar mhaith leat deoch?'
'Níl cead agam.'

'I'm not allowed.' So I told her to leave it with me, and I had a Britvic Orange with a hint of vodka in it waiting for her when she was finished playing. I eventually got the nerve to ask her to dance, and we danced a full Clare set together ... well, I attempted to dance it and Dympna glided around the room. Clare women are the best set dancers in the country; it's in their bones. The set lasted 20 minutes, and by the end of it I was *faoi gheasa aici*. Smitten.

And the rest is history. Little did I know that in a few years I'd be marrying into the greatest *céilí* band of all times, the Kilfenora Céilí Band, the Rolling Stones of Irish traditional music.

Mo stór, a stór mo chroí, mo mhuirnín
My love, treasure of my heart, my beloved

[muh store, a store muh khree, muh wurn-een]

An bhfuil tú ag mothú ceart go leor, mo stór?
Are you feeling well, my love?

> *You can see a woman standing on the local pier crying because her beloved is lost at sea.*

You find these phrases in nearly every Irish love song. Connemara songs seem to be either about sadness and emigration or love and craic. These words are used for high levels of emotion and sadness, real tear-jerker stuff. Even in words like this that are about love, you can feel the pain. You can see a woman standing on the local pier crying because her beloved is lost at sea, or an old woman sitting by the stove with a nip of *poitín* singing a *sean-nós* song about all those who have left for America, and the whole kitchen is silent, and the moonlight is shining on the thatched cottage. Proper postcard scenes for beautiful old phrases.

There's a sense of longing for people who have gone far away in these words, or they can be said by a parent cradling their little baby because they're upset. They're just three beautiful ways to talk about somebody who means so much to you.

Tá mé fiáin agat
I'm mad about you/wild for you

[taw may fee-awn att]

An rachaidh tú amach liom?
Cén fáth?
Mar tá mé fiáin agat!
Will you go out with me?
Why?
Because I'm wild about you!

Even the tides couldn't stop women going wild for Freddy.

My brother Freddy was a popular man with the ladies. Freddy was a bit of a *staic* (page 222), a good-looking fella.

He would pick me and the lads up in his car on a Saturday night and we would head off to a nightclub. The sounds of Soundgarden and Pearl Jam playing and a flagon of cider between us in the back. When we got there, Freddy would disappear for an hour or two and arrive back with a girl on his arm. It wasn't unusual for him to go home with someone and for the rest of us to be standing in the chipper getting a snack box at two o'clock in the morning, me wondering how the hell I was going to get home.

There would always be the knock on my bedroom door the next morning: my mother.

'Where's Freddy?'
'I don't know.'
'Well, the car's not there.'

One Sunday it got to lunch and there was still no sign of him. He'd missed the Sunday roast and there was no way to check in with him to see if he was okay. Then, at seven o'clock that evening, Freddy arrives home with his car on the back of a tow truck, seaweed coming out of the doors. He'd driven all the way to Bettystown for a skinny-dip with the girl he'd met. They'd fallen asleep in the car and woke up with the tide back in and the pedals submerged in water. Even the tides couldn't stop women going wild for Freddy. We should have nicknamed him *'Freddy Fiáin'*.

So this is a shout-out to my brother Freddy and to all the good-looking brothers and sisters who never had to ask for the shift. They dominated the discos of Ireland while the rest of us were standing at the bar, trying to order a pint.

Réiltín
Little star

[rail-teen]

Is réiltín thú.
You're a little star.

A term for a child who's done you a good turn, like your daughter running out to the car to get in the last bag of shopping.

'*Réiltín*' is a great example of the power of '*-ín*' in Irish. It can be added to almost anything to make it a term of endearment, so 'little dote' would be '*dóitín*'. It's even worked its way into English as 'een' at the end of words. I use the word 'loveen' daily in Galway, especially when I go to Mary's Fish Shop in Ballybane to get fish on a Friday. I walk in and all I hear from behind the counter is 'How're ya Hector loveen?' What a beautiful way to start a conversation.

'*Réiltín*' is a perfect term for a child who's done you a good turn, like your daughter running out to the car to get in the last bag of shopping or the 12-year-old you've sent out in the rain to get a bucket of coal even though you wouldn't set foot outside the door yourself. Anything good we did in our house in Navan, our mam would call us a 'little topper'. 'Go out and take the clothes off the line there, you little topper.' It was a lovely, warm way to tell us we'd done a great job.

Cuimil
Soft rubbing of the hand

[cwi-mil]

Chuimil sé mo lámh.
He rubbed my hand.

> *A husband picking up his wife's hand and holding it to say, 'I'm with you.'*

You would use *cuimil* on only special occasions. It's the action of rubbing someone's hand softly to comfort them. You see it at gravesides, at sickbeds, when someone is feeling low or has experienced a loss. It's a verb with a soft pronunciation that creates a strong image: a husband picking up his wife's hand and holding it to say, 'I'm with you,' or a son or daughter looking after their elderly parents.

I don't know of a word in English that does the same job, and 'rub' doesn't do it justice. It's one of those Irish terms that can hardly be translated, because it's all about the doing of it – reaching out the warm hand of affection. The action you use when there are no words to say.

Tá sí slachtmhar
She is pretty

[taw she slakht-ver]

Tá an seomra glan agus slachtmhar.
The room is clean and tidy.

> *The language of cleanliness co-opted to the language of love.*

You're on a stag night in the Aran Islands and you're sitting in one corner of Tí Joe Wattys and there's a hen party in the other. You're having a sneaky look over at the hens and you spot someone who takes your fancy, so you elbow your friend and say, 'Jesus, Dave, will you look at yer one. *Tá sí slachtmhar.*' '*Slachtmhar*' is the word for 'tidy', so you're literally saying, 'Your one over there is tidy.' It is the language of cleanliness co-opted to the language of love.

You can use it in a straightforward way to say 'tidy' as well, like the little jig you do around your living room with the Hoover when the in-laws text to say they're in the area and sure they'll drop in for a cup of tea. This is a high-level Irish way to describe somebody who has caught your eye, or to describe that person you know who is so tidy and organised that they even colour-code their socks.

SEVEN

Words for the back of your knee and other body parts

Irish bodies are different to everyone else's bodies. They just are. They have been shaped by the wind and the rain, the soil and the stone walls. There's no way we could ever look like people from the mainland of Europe. You can imagine me emigrating to Bilbao in 1992 and heading down to the beach for a swim. My skin was iridescent. I had more in common with the jellyfish than the people. Irish bodies are made to be hidden away. That's why we invented the Aran jumper.

It's our lines of latitude and longitude that have given us bodies that are usually only ever seen by the light of a lava lamp in student accommodation. So it's a wonder we have such lovely Irish words for very specific parts of the body. There's a word for the back of the knee – that part above the welly line and below GAA short territory that you rarely think about. Then there's the word for freckles – two words, actually – that describes these tiny marks on our skin as celestial.

I think as a nation we'd sometimes prefer to pretend we don't have bodies at all, but our language tells a different tale: we have *barraicíní* (page 256) for dancing and *ascaill* (page 254) for hugging and *roic* (page 246) that tell the story of our lives.

Bricíní/póigíní gréine
Freckles

[brick-een-ee/po-gee-nee gray-nya]

Is breá liom na póigíní gréine a fuair tú agus tú ag taisteal!
I love the freckles you got while travelling!

The Irish arm is a blank canvas that's painted when the sun kisses our skin, and every arm is different.

When you talk about someone's freckles in Irish, whether you choose *bricíní* or *póigíní gréine*, it's automatically a compliment. These words also mean 'little stars' (*bricíní*) and 'little sun kisses' (*póigíní gréine*). 'Freckles' in English could go either way – it sounds like a word that could have been invented by the HSE. But how beautiful to think of tiny pieces of stars on your skin! There's even a myth that they come from the ancient gods sprinkling stardust on us as a reminder of the galaxies above our heads.

Some of us have just a few freckles, some of us have loads, and we redheads probably have entire constellations. I've got a smattering on my arms and hands, like small broken bits of Corn Flakes. It's definitely something deep in the genes of the red-haired and fair-skinned. The mad thing is that none of us have freckles when we're born into the world; we collect them as we grow up. The Irish arm is a blank canvas that's painted when the sun kisses our skin, and every arm is different. Is there anything more beautiful than the *póigíní gréine* you get across your nose after a warm summer spent outdoors? I'll take the Irish words above 'freckles' any day of the week. *Meas mór ag dul amach go dtí an bricíní* posse!

Roic
Wrinkles

[rick]

Bhí éadán an iascaire lán le roic théis a shaol a chaitheamh ar an uisce.
The face of the fisherman was wrinkled after a life spent out on the water.

The wrinkles of your grandparents tell you that they love you and to put on your coat because it's cold outside.

I think wrinkles are magnificent, but we have become ashamed of what wrinkles bring. I think our *roic* should be celebrated. Wrinkles bring knowledge, they bring character, they tell stories, and they make smiles. Wrinkles drink porter and wrinkles give hugs. The wrinkles of your grandparents tell you that they love you and to put on your coat because it's cold outside. There are wrinkles in nature – in the ripples of water and in the patterns of a ploughed field. They are little vibrations written onto our faces and onto the land. I love the wrinkles all around me, on the faces of my family and friends.

You can look at someone's face and know they've laughed thousands of times. Just look at Samuel Beckett, one of the great Irish faces. You know there are stories there. It makes me happy to know that every time I smile, my face records it in a laughter line. They're like a map of the funny stories I've heard.

Roic are the lines of our lives, and I think we should love them instead of trying to get rid of them, because if you take away your wrinkles it's like taking away your DNA. They're little fadas on our faces.

Uillinn
Elbow

[ill-in]

Níl faitíos uirthi uillinn a thabhairt dá hiomaitheoirí ar an bpáirc.
She's well able to give the elbow when she's out on the pitch.

> *I want to set the record straight and say that I was into Elbow well before they ever played in Ireland.*

Elbow are one of my favourite bands of all time. I want to set the record straight and say that I was into Elbow well before they ever played in Ireland. When my boys were small, and we'd be driving in the car, I used to put on Elbow for them every day. One of their albums way back was called *Asleep in the Back*, so I thought it was a great one for them sitting in the back of the car, nodding their little heads. I used to tell them what 'elbow' is in Irish, so *'uillinn'* has always made me think of that music.

The uilleann pipes get their name from the movement of the elbow when playing the instrument, which is something that most people will know. And I can't think of the uilleann pipes without thinking of Davy Spillane, the great Irish musician. He's the Jimi Hendrix of the uilleann pipes. When you think of 'uilleann' in relation to music, it takes on a different meaning.

Of course, an *uillinn* is just a body part that you wouldn't give a second thought to, unless you hurt it, which I learned well when my son Shane was seven and he came into the house with a floppy arm after trying to dive off a collapsible stool into a paddling pool. Myself and the wife had been enjoying the hurling final with a bottle of Santa Rita, which was dropped for a bottle of Calpol when we saw him. And then Shane, his broken *uillinn* and Daddy were off to the hospital in the car, and I knew the perfect band to provide the soundtrack for the journey.

Straois
Smirk

[streesh]

Bain an straois sin de d'aghaidh.
Take that smirk off your face.

The know-it-all smirking and sneering down the back of the class.

I want all the teachers in the country to know this word. It's a great one for cheeky teenagers: the know-it-all smirking and sneering down the back of the class. Just make sure to deliver it with passion and stretch the pronunciation: 'streeeesh'. 'Raymond Flaherty/Colin O'Brien/Maria Deveraux, *bain an straois sin de d'agahaidh*.' Boom!

I'm sure I was told many a time to take the smirk off my face back in the day in St Pat's in Navan. I wasn't cheeky, but I was a giddy young messer in school. The favourite punishment of teachers in the '80s was to throw you out of class if you misbehaved, and you'd be standing outside hoping and praying the principal, Spud Murphy, wouldn't walk by and see you. The more trouble you were in, the longer the ban would be. It could be the 40 minutes of class or it could be a week – I even got thrown out of French class for a whole year. Luckily, I never took much to the language anyway. If that happened now, I'm sure there would be a small court tribunal, but back then the teachers had the power and I salute them. I would have thrown me and my *straois* out of the class as well.

Ioscaid
Back of the knee

[iss-coid]

Beidh mé sna hioscaidí agat.
I'll be right behind you/I'll back you all the way!

The hidden valley, the Glendalough of the leg – you've probably been there once, but you didn't really get to see it and you can't remember much about it.

The back of the knee is an underrated, almost forgotten part of the body. Like they say, 'out of sight, out of mind', unless you're unlucky enough to get sunburnt on the back of the legs and then it'll be all you can think about. *'Ioscaid'* is the hidden valley, the Glendalough of the leg – you've probably been there once, but you didn't really get to see it and you can't remember much about it. But if you unfold your leg, there's a whole world back there.

The front of the knee in Irish is *'glúin'*, which interestingly is also the word for 'generation'. So when you say *'ó ghlúin go glúin'*, from generation to generation, you're also saying 'from knee to knee'. *'Ioscaid'*, though, is a fairly new word for me, but I'm delighted I've learned it so I can teach you this very specific word for a very specific part of the body. I'm sure there is a medical term for the back of the knee in English that only orthopaedic surgeons use, but *'ioscaid'* is an everyday, normal word in Irish.

If you look at the sentence on the opposite page, you'll see *'ioscaid'* can be used to say you're backing someone, that you're going to be behind them. So this is a word for a rarely-thought-about body part that's also used to say you have someone's back, that you are there to support them. Irish can take a word for one simple thing, repurpose it, and let it take flight.

Ascaill
Underarm/armpit

[aws-kill]

Chuir sí a lámh i m'ascaill agus shiúil muid linn ón séipéal.
We linked arms as we walked together from the church.

It's the part we use to link each other as we walk, so to me it means connection.

'*Ascaill*' is the word for the underside of your arm and your armpit in Irish. The word for 'arm' in general is '*lámh*', which also means 'hand', or '*géag*', which means 'branch'. I love that Irish uses the same word for 'arm' as it does for 'branch', but I've chosen '*ascaill*' here because it's so specifically the underside of the arm. It's the part we use to link each other as we walk, so to me it means connection. There was a time when holding hands and linking arms was a big thing, but you don't see it as often anymore. I love seeing a son or daughter linking arms with their mam or dad. It's a sign of love and respect. It's a quick way of showing affection and support, like linking arms with someone as they leave a funeral, as if to say, 'I'll take your weight.' It's a part of the body that expresses a lot of feeling.

'*Ascaill*' is also the word for 'avenue' in Irish. You'll see hundreds of '*ascaills*' as you drive around Dublin – *Ascaill Uí Ghríofa, Ascaill Bhaile Bhailcín, Ascaill Foster* – and it won't have anything to do with armpits. I'm not sure how they are related, but I wouldn't be surprised if some guy called Des Moriarty in Dublin City Council came up with the idea to use '*ascaill*' for 'avenue' in 1926, and now when we hear the word we probably think of street names before we think about the power of offering someone your arm in support.

Barraicíní
Toes

[bar-rack-ee-nee]

Sáil agus barraicín, a haon, a dó, a trí ...
Heel and toe, with the one, two, three ...

> *What a great way to learn words for parts of the body, swinging each other around a hall to 'Seáinín' on a balmy summer's night, wondering if you'll get the shift later.*

'*Barraicíní*' is one of the first words I learned in Irish. That might sound odd, but it's because of all the steps I had to learn for the céilís in the Gaeltacht. And, by God, did you learn the dances properly in Coláiste na bhFiann.

From the first few days into my Gaeltacht odyssey, I was lepping around a hall trying to follow the teachers' instructions. First we had to learn the most famous of the Gaeltacht dances, 'The Walls of Limerick'. It's the backbone of the *halla*; no *céilí* is complete, from Donegal to Kerry, without '*Ballaí Luimnigh*'. Then we graduated to 'The Siege of Ennis', and when the hundred or so 12- to 15-year-olds grasped that, it was on to '*Seáinín*', or 'Johnny' in English. I can still hear the rhythm and air in my head: '*Sáil agus barraicín, a haon, a dó, a trí, iompaigh ... sáil agus barraicín, a haon, a dó, a trí, iompaigh!*' We were all bashing off each other, trying to keep up, and the *cúntóirí* would be jigging around us, shouting, 'HEEL AND TOE, ONE, TWO, THREE, TURN!' It was *Strictly Come Dancing, céilí* style in 1983. And what a great way to learn words for parts of the body, swinging each other around a hall to '*Seáinín*' on a balmy summer's night, wondering if you'll get the shift later.

Sramaí
Sleep (in eyes)

[shraa-mwee]

Bhí cuma thuirseach air, bhí sramaí ar a shúile.
He looked tired, he had sleep in his eyes.

The yellow stuff you find in the corners of your eyes in the morning.

'*Sramaí*' is the Irish word for the yellow stuff you find in the corners of your eyes in the morning. I was fascinated by the lads at school who always seemed to have bits of yellow gunk in their eyes and never wiped it off. I couldn't bear it. I was practically reaching out the hand to wipe it away myself. The people who get the yellow *sramaí* on their eyelashes too must be getting well over the eight hours a night. It's as if their eyes are glued together with sleep Bostik.

My mother wouldn't let us out of the door with even a hint of it on our eyes. Now if I see any sign of it on my two boys, I'm on it like a rash. We called *sramaí* 'duck's feet' in my house. I don't know if it's a west of Ireland thing or a family thing, because the first time I heard someone call it 'sleep' I thought they were mad, and they thought I was mad for calling it 'duck's feet'. But it's a good thing there's a word for it in Irish, so we can all just call it '*sramaí*'.

Gogaide
Squat/hunkers

[gug-a-dja]

Gabh síos ar do ghogaide.
Go down on your hunkers.

You might get down on your gogaide
to talk to a small child.

M y mam used to use this word at home in Navan with us all the time. She was born 10 miles from Tuam, and she would have heard it as a child growing up in rural north Galway. Then she passed it on to us. She didn't speak Irish – none of my family did – but it was used around her when she was growing up, so little bits of the language worked their way into her daily life. It's interesting how this word reached out across Connemara, over Lough Corrib, and into her part of Galway. Throughout the years, these Irish words were knitted into the English spoken by the locals. Shadows of *Gaeilge* that lingered even though more and more people started to speak English as their first language.

It's a beautiful word, and it sounds much nicer than 'hunkers'. A hen lays eggs on her *gogaide*, *'bíonn cearc ar a gogaide ag breith uibhe'*. You might get down on your *gogaide* to talk to a small child. In fact, in another lovely example of the interconnectedness of Irish, the word *'gogamán'*, meaning babysitter or childminder, comes from *'gogaide'*.

Fabhraí agus malaí
Eyelashes and eyebrows

[fow-ree aw-gus maw-lee]

D'fhéach mé faoi na fabhraí air.
I stole a glance at him.

Níor leag mé fabhra aréir.
Didn't sleep a wink last night.

> *Something deep in our Irish genes has produced a nation of people with long eyelashes and spectacular eyebrows.*

'*Fabhraí*' and '*malaí*' aren't words you're going to learn in Irish in school, but they're great ones to know because something deep in our Irish genes has produced a nation of people with long eyelashes and spectacular eyebrows. Eyelashes get all the focus at Bonny Baby competitions around the country, but I think eyebrows should be given more attention. We have great eyebrows as a nation, big bushy yokes that give off an air of magnificence:

> The thespian eyebrows of Brendan Gleeson
> The football eyebrows of Jim McGuinness
> The literary eyebrows of Brendan Behan
> The musical eyebrows of Luke Kelly
> The presidential eyebrows of Michael D. Higgins.

They are the Great Eyebrows of Ireland and they should be celebrated. The bands the Dubliners and the Fureys were each like a collective eyebrow. The secret to success must be pints, eyebrows, more pints and traditional ballads.

There's big money in the eyelash and eyebrow industry now, but if you walked into a barber in Navan in the '70s in your pinstripe suit and said, 'And will you give my eyebrows a little trim as well?', the barber would slap the face off you. If you want to let your eyebrows run wild, let them run wild. I guarantee you people with bushy eyebrows have stories to tell.

Na maotháin
Earlobes

[na mway-hawn]

Chuir sí na fáinní cluaise ina maotháin cluaise.
She put the earrings into her earlobes.

> *I became obsessed with cleaning my ears the first time my mother put the Johnson & Johnson cotton bud tub into the lemon-coloured press in the bathroom.*

As parts of the body goes, I've a fair aul liking for earlobes. They're the softest part of the body. Their texture reminds me of the curtains we had in our front room in 1976. We had one good room where the television was and where the uncles and aunties sat when they came over at Christmastime. But it was freezing, so my mother got purple velvet curtains to save the heat, and I thought that it was the future. I'd never felt something so soft in my life. We had Navan carpet, velvet curtains, and one of those little drinks trolleys. I thought we were posh.

In contrast to the lobes, a dirty ear is one of my pet hates. There are ears in some parishes around the country that haven't been cleaned in decades. I became obsessed with cleaning my ears the first time my mother put the Johnson & Johnson cotton bud tub into the lemon-coloured press in the bathroom. It was my mother's job to clean our ears after the bath on a Saturday night, and sometimes she would say, 'Gimme a look in them ears ... Ohhh Jesus, you could plant spuds in them!' Once I hit my teens, it was my turn. I'd lock the bathroom door, stand there, and poke my ears with the buds, sensations exploding all around my head. Then I'd check how much gunk I'd extracted before tossing the bud in the bin and going for a fresh one. By the time I was 16 I was well into the ear buds. It was a daily ritual; even when I knew my ears were clean, I'd still go at it. I still love a good-quality, pristine bud; sure my *maotháin* deserve it.

Daitheacha(í)
Awful bad toothache

[doy-ya-kha]

Fuair mé suaimhneas na daitheacha théis dom cuairt a thabhairt ar an bhfiaclóir.
I got relief from the toothache after visiting the dentist.

Our ancestors probably chewed bark to relieve the pain.

When I was around twelve, I had to get braces. I got four teeth removed, had the braces put on, and left the dentist not being able to pronounce my Ss properly. I had just gone into first year in secondary school and I was really embarrassed. I think my family DNA has given me decent gnashers. Luckily we don't suffer from too many toothaches in my house, but there's no doubt we've been dealing with toothaches in Ireland for millennia.

Our ancestors probably chewed the bark of a certain tree to relieve the pain. On my travels, I've seen people using twigs from certain trees to clean their teeth, almost like a natural toothpaste. In Ireland, if we have a problem with our mouth, we use the good old Bonjela. There's not a household in the country without a tube of Bonjela and a tub of Sudocrem. Gripe water, however ... now that's contraband. You can't get it anymore but it's great for a toothache. There's a black market for the stuff in the Republic. It used to be for green diesel, but now it's gripe water. Desperate parents with colicky babies driving to the North to smuggle a couple of bottles across the border. Now you can probably message gripe water dealers on Instagram 24 hours a day to get you a bottle.

A toothache is an awful thing, and *daitheacha* is the Irish word for one that's really, really bad. It probably came from a time when dentists weren't a thing so it was hard to get relief. Even so, there are still people out there with toothaches who think dentists are good but whiskey is better.

Cloigeann
The head

[klig-in]

Tá cloigeann tinn orm.
I've a sore head.

Used most often in relation to a hangover.

'*Cloigeann*' is a word you can only use when your head is sore. It's no mistake that it's more or less the same word for 'bell' in Irish, '*cloigín*', because it's used most often in relation to a hangover.

The first time I heard this word, I was in a pub in Inis Meáin and someone was singing '*Mé Féin is mo Mhéit*'. Everyone in Connemara knows this song – it's the 'Ring of Fire' of Irish tunes.

It was a Saturday night and there was going to be live music in the local pub. We were hosting the legends of Connemara John Beag Ó Flatharta and his band na hAncairí, supported by Sonny Choilm Learaí, an icon of the Irish music scene from Leitir Mealláin. The pub was packed, the door was open all night with the heat, and the rich sounds of Connemara floated around the roads of Inis Meáin.

It was the first time I'd heard '*Mé Féin is mo Mhéit*', a beautiful sad story of a young man who left the west of Ireland for London in search of work but dreamt of being back home. When John Beag hit the chorus, the pub broke out in song. This was their anthem, people who had all felt the pain of emigration at their kitchen tables. The song has a gorgeous folky feel to it, and the lyrics have stuck with me. I really understood what it was like to have a '*cloigeann tinn*' when I heard them, especially the line '*Ar phócaí folmha is cloigeann tinn*' (empty pockets and a sore head).

Smut
Nose/snout

[smut]

Bhuail mé sa smut é.
I smacked him straight in his snout.

That point on the tip of your nose, smack bang in the centre of your face.

Right on the button. '*Smut*' is the Irish word for that point on the tip of your nose, smack bang in the centre of your face. It's like in comic books when you see Batman punch a baddie and it says 'KAPOW!' Boxers use jabs all the time; it's the go-to shot in a fight, whether it's an under-14s bout in the National Stadium or Katie Taylor defending her world title in Madison Square Garden. They all want that jab landing right on the *smut*.

It's a great phrase to keep up your sleeve for when you're watching boxing, but you can also use it when you're training in your puppy and you might give him a little tip on the snout.

EIGHT

Upgrade your Irish insults

'Eejit' is one of the most common 'nice' insults we have in the English language, and there are a million ways to call someone an eejit in Irish. There is a whole scale of eejitry, and your tone of voice will give away which level of eejit you're referring to. There's an eejit driving the brand-new Range Rover in front of you at the school drop-off, there's an eejit ordering a chicken fillet roll in the garage, and there's an eejit sitting at the desk across from you in work. Some eejits you can't stand, some eejits are harmless, and sometimes you're an eejit yourself.

This chapter is full of phrases that will upgrade your Irish insults. There are words for when your small child is acting the maggot, perfect for a domestic situation. And then there are the old Irish curses … These are not to be taken lightly. They are powerful and imaginative ways to wish pain on your enemy. Some of them sound like there's ancient magic in them, calling down the wrath of God, and others are just about hoping someone gets diarrhoea. I don't know which is worse.

A phleidhce
Ya messer

[a fly-ka]

Bhí mé i mo phleidhce mór nuair a bhí mé ar scoil.
I used to be an awful messer when I was at school.

*An insult said with a hint of
a smile on your face.*

If there was an honours degree in messing, I'd have a masters. I learned the phrase *'ag pleidhcíocht'*, 'messing', fairly quickly in my first summer at the Gaeltacht. When you have 16 teenagers from all over the country, giddy after coming back from the evening *céilí*, all trying to brush their teeth at the same time and then sleep in bunk beds, that's a recipe for messing of the highest level. If you put a group of teenagers in a room with bunk beds, what are they going to do? Read a book? Go to sleep? Not a chance. Bunk beds are *craic* beds.

This is generally the point when the *cúntóir* would come in and shout, 'Come on, *ciúnas anois! Stop an phleidhcíocht, leaids!*' at us. The *cúntóirí* loved the power they wielded over their group of hormonal teenagers, so we heard *'pleidhcíocht'* at least twice a day.

I've included *'a phleidhce'* in the bad words chapter, but I actually think being a messer is admired in Ireland, so it's really a compliment. An insult said with a hint of a smile on your face.

A leibide
Ya buffoon/idiot

[a leb-i-ja]

Céard a rinne tú leis an gcarr? Chuir tú unleaded *isteach in ionad* diesel, *a leibide!*
What did you do with the car? You put in unleaded instead of diesel, ya eejit!

Just a bit of an idiot, a harmless buffoon.

You might know the word *'amadán'*, which you would use for someone who doesn't really have much going on upstairs, but a *leibide* is just a bit of an idiot, a harmless buffoon. There's no real malice in it. You might say it to a friend: 'What did you go and buy me a birthday present for, ya *leibide*?'

We will all do something from time to time that brings us to the *leibide* level on the scale of eejitry. Even me. For example, we have homemade chips almost every Friday in our house, and I'm the only one who's allowed to move the chip pan. It's a big, old-style chip fryer that's basically a big box of oil. When we're finished our dinner, I transport it back into the utility room because it's a Dad Job. If anyone else moved it they might spill the oil everywhere. So one Friday the cord got caught in the door as I was moving it, it yanked the fryer, and every bit of oil spilled on top of me and all over the floor. Then the dog came in to investigate and he was skating all over the place like Torvill and Dean. And I was shouting, 'Get out, get out, get out!' to our little Jack Russell doing pirouettes. That made my son Shane come in to see what was wrong, and he started skating on the oily floor as well. It took the force of 10 *Sunday Times* newspapers to clean it up. I was an idiot, but thankfully being a *leibide* is a temporary state.

A phleota
Ya fool

[a float-a]

Rinne tú dearmad ar an gumshield *arís, a phleota?*
Did you forget your gumshield again, ya eejit?

It's a word for the 'I told you so' moments that parents of teenagers can't resist.

'*Aphleota*' is another level on the scale of eejitry. It would be used most often in domestic situations, when a carefree child comes into contact with a cranky parent. It's like trying to get a teenager to wear a jacket, one of life's most impossible tasks. You might be able to service a ride-on lawnmower but you still wouldn't be able to get a 16-year-old to put on a coat in the middle of winter. They will come home from school with a head cold and Mommy will turn around and say, 'Well? What did I tell you? It's freezing. You should have worn a jacket, a *phleota*.' It's a word for the 'I told you so' moments that parents of teenagers can't resist.

Lúdramán
Idler/lazy good for nothing

[loo-dra-mawn]

Ó a dhiabhail, is lúdramán ceart thú. Bhí an t-agallamh sin ar siúl inniu, ní amárach!
Oh, my God, you're an awful idiot. That interview was on today, not tomorrow!

A classic insult you would hear coming out of the mouth of a teacher if a child was trying to eat marla.

'*Lúdramán*' is a real school-yard word. It's a classic insult you would hear coming out of the mouth of a teacher if a child was trying to eat *marla*. A *lúdramán* isn't a great thing to be called, but it's still not as bad as calling someone a 'dunce' or, in my case, a 'mathematical cripple'.

There were plenty of insults going around in St Pat's in Navan in the '80s, and I was a bit of a *lúdramán* in secondary school when it came to maths. My teacher christened me a 'mathematical cripple' and I was sent down the back of the class to do my Irish. So while everyone else was calculating percentages, I was conjugating verbs.

I managed to get an E in pass maths in the Leaving Cert. I went into the exam and instead of doing it, I read the log book because there was Irish on the back and it passed a bit of time, then I left after about thirty minutes. But even though I was a *lúdramán* in maths, I still managed to get into Trinity because I got an honour in Latin.

Raiméis/seafóid
Bullshit

[ra-maysh/sha-foyd]

Ná bí ag caint seafóide.
Don't be talking bullshit.

The politicians and CEOs on Prime Time *who talk an absolute mile of muck.*

I have to give a nod to English here, because 'bullshit' is a fantastic word. I don't know where it's derived from – I've never seen a bull having a poo – but it's one of the great swearwords in English that everyone should use. It's a useful adjective in a country full of bullshitters.

'*Raiméis*' is used for the top-level bullshitters – the politicians and CEOs on *Prime Time* who talk an absolute mile of muck. When I say it, I can see two Connemara men standing on the sidelines of the Leitir Mealláin GAA pitch giving out about the utter *raiméis* the ref just pulled in the match.

'*Seafóid*', on the other hand, would be used for your friend who's talking absolute shite down the pub. It's a softer level of bullshit. They might be waffling on about how they'd definitely be able to beat Serena Williams in a game of tennis and the only way to shut them up is to say, 'Would you give it up, that's complete *seafóid*. Last time you played tennis they had wooden rackets.'

We're great at calling out *seafóid* with our friends, but we need to get better at calling out *raiméis* from the government because we've gone well beyond our quota at this stage.

A shuarachán
Ya scut

[A hoo-ra-khawn]

Stop ag éalú ó Mhamaí, a shuarachán.
Stop running away from Mammy, ya little scut.

> *They can't resist running up to the altar in mass when the priest has his head shoved in the tabernacle.*

'A*shuarachán*' is a harmless phrase that you would use for those energetic kids you see out and about causing mayhem. Formal occasions bring the best out of *suaracháin*. They can't resist running up to the altar in mass when the priest has his head shoved in the tabernacle, or making a break for it in a restaurant when Mammy and Daddy are too distracted by their lasagna to stop them.

When I say 'scut', I can almost hear my mother saying it. I'd say she called me a 'little scut' at least once a day. It's an affectionate phrase for a curious child who unintentionally causes a bit of mischief, and I was definitely one of those. It's a phrase that lives in harmony with everyday life. 'Come here to me, ya *suarachán*!'

Cladhaire
Coward, chicken

[kleye-ra]

Maidir le huisce domhain, is cladhaire mór mé.
When it comes to deep water, I'm an awful chicken.

I didn't learn to swim until I was 28, but thankfully I got over my fear of kissing girls much earlier than that.

When was the last time you were called a chicken or a coward? It was probably in school. This is a phrase you would hear when a friend dares you to do something but you're too afraid so you chicken out. You're usually reluctant out of a good sense of self-preservation, but that doesn't matter to your mates. When I was a kid, a fella in my neighbourhood dared me to kiss Fidelma down the road but I was too scared. 'Ahhh, are ya afraid? Ya big chicken.' Not exactly life-threatening, but at that age you may as well have been asking me to jump in a river.

I've done a lot of scary and dangerous things on my travel show: I've hung out of the side of a helicopter, I've flown on a microlight over the Victoria Falls, I've taken a rickety cable car up a mountain in Eastern Europe in the middle of winter, I've wandered the Amazon jungle for six weeks. There's not much I'm afraid of, but I'm always a chicken when it comes to deep water, all because an older lad in Navan pushed me into a pool when I was six years old. I didn't learn to swim until I was 28, but thankfully I got over my fear of kissing girls much earlier than that. Now I'll dive into the deep end of a pool no problem, but when it comes to deep, open water, I'm still a *cladhaire*.

Cé thú féin anyways?
Who are you anyways?

[kay hoo fain anyays?]

Haigh, céard atá tú ag déanamh? Bhris tú an solas dearg.
Fuckáil leat! Cé thú féin anyways?
Hey, what are you at? You broke the red light!
Fuck you. Who are you anyways?

> *Went viral when a road rage video was posted online, spreading the phrase from a small road in Connemara across every county in Ireland.*

In Ireland, everyone knows everyone, or at least they know someone who might know them, so 'Who are you anyways?' is a great insult. It's also the most modern phrase in the book with the bit of English thrown in.

It's fairly common in Connemara for someone to say, *'Cé thú féin* anyways?', but it went viral when a road rage video was posted online, spreading the phrase from a small road in Connemara across every county in Ireland.

A van driver and a car driver had an altercation that started with beeping horns and quickly escalated to them pulling up beside each other and letting fly. The quality of the Irish language was obvious from the word go, with a barrage of insults and curses going back and forth ... and then *'Cé thú fuckin' féin* anyways?' was born. Within 24 hours the video had tens of thousands of views on X, then the WhatsApp groups got hold of it and away it went. The nation had a new insult in the purest of pure Connemara *blas*.

I had the pleasure of meeting the mother of the lad who spat out the *'Cé thú fuckin' féin* anyways?' in Galway a few months after the video was doing the rounds, and she couldn't be prouder. Her son was a legend in every household in the country. It was poetry in motion.

Mallacht Dé ort
The curse of God on you

[maw-lokht day urt]

Tá tú ag féachaint ar Lord of the Rings *as Gaeilge ar TG4, agus tá Gandalf ar an sliabh ag screadaíl, 'Mallacht Dé ort!'*
You're watching Lord of the Rings as Gaeilge on TG4, and there's Gandalf on the mountain shouting, 'The curse of God on you!'

You can imagine your great-grandparents saying this on a road in Connemara in 1921, bringing the wrath of God onto their enemy.

Ohhh, there's venom in this one alright. To use God is the highest of high curses, so it doesn't get much stronger than this. You can imagine your great-grandparents saying this on a road in Connemara in 1921, bringing the wrath of God onto their enemy when the Church was practically omnipotent and priests ruled the parish. You know your grandmother means business when she uses a profanity or brings the Lord into it.

Profanities invoking God have dwindled along with congregation numbers, so this is an old-timer's curse. But it's still one that weighs heavily on your tongue, meant to inflict damage and badness. I've never used it, but I respect the fury and anger that comes with it. They're actually calling on God to come down with fire and brimstone and blast you off the face of the earth. It's not something you would say to someone who skipped you in a queue; only deep, generational anger can bring this one out.

Go dtachta an diabhal thú!
May the devil strangle/choke you!

[gu jakh-takh on jowal who]

Sin mo thalamh ansin, sin é an teorainn. Cuir suas balla ansin agus brisfidh mé é roimh mhaidin.
Tá tú go dona, go dtachta an diabhal thú!
That's my land there, there's the boundary. Put a wall up there and I'll knock it down by morning.
You're a bad bit of work you are, may the devil strangle you!

There's blood and there's bitterness and there's tension buried in this insult.

Curses like this wield power. It's not for someone who didn't buy their round in the pub or forgot to order you chips with your meal. There's blood and there's bitterness and there's tension buried in this insult. Something really bad must have happened if you say this. To wish someone to be strangled is bad enough, but bringing the devil into it is another thing entirely.

If you were leaving your local pub in Connemara in 1956, and there was an old woman at the gate as you walked by with a pint of Guinness and *poitín* in your belly, and she said to you, 'Go dtachta an diabhal thú,' you'd be running home and locking the doors. It's horror movie stuff.

I don't know if it's worse to have the curse of the devil or the curse of God (page 290) brought upon you, but whatever was happening in Connemara centuries ago to have people come up with these insults must have been monumental.

Loscadh is dó ort
Scorching and burning on you

[lus-ca iss dough ort]

Céard a dúirt tú; ní bhfuair tú na málaí tae?
Loscadh is dó ort!
What do you mean you didn't get the teabags?
Scorching and burning on you!

Gandalf-level cursing, standing on the top of a hill to stop the armies of darkness.

This brings me back to four o'clock on a Wednesday afternoon watching RTÉ and He-Man comes on, lifts his sword to the sky, and says, 'By the power of GRAYSKULL, I HAVE THE POWER!' It is all about calling down fire and brimstone, real Biblical stuff. It is Gandalf-level cursing, standing on the top of a hill to stop the armies of darkness.

What kind of situation would you have to be in to say 'scorching and burning on you' to someone? There's so much anger in it. It would have to be Richard Harris in *The Field* cursing his neighbour, or a spat between two farming families that caused a lot of tension to be passed down from generation to generation, but then you find out it started because their great-great-grandfather kicked your great-great-grandfather in the shin.

It's not something you would necessarily use a lot these days, but if you do, you have to raise your arm to the sky like He-Man: 'By the power of ANNASCAUL, *LOSCADH IS DÓ ORT!*'

Briseadh agus brú ort
Strife and stress on you

[brish-a aw-gus broo urt]

Céard a rinne tú? Cheannaigh tú Barry's tae?
Briseadh agus brú ort!
What did you do? You bought *Barry's* tea?
Strife and stress on you!

Channel your inner Jackie Healy-Rae and shout it at your husband in the kitchen when he's missed the bins AGAIN.

This insult is Shakespearean. When you read this, it has to be in a deep, resounding voice. Channel your inner Jackie Healy-Rae and shout it at your husband in the kitchen when he's missed the bins AGAIN for another week. It is about inflicting complete and utter mayhem on someone. Even saying the word 'strife' makes me feel stressed.

'Briseadh agus brú' literally translates to 'breaking and pressing/crushing', and the phrase seems to come from *'briseadh agus brú ar do chnámha'*, 'may your bones break and crush'. You are calling down a stress on someone so big that their bones crush under the weight of it. It is a stressful phrase for a stressful situation, and a great one for a family feud. 'You left your wet towels on the floor again, for Jaysis' sake. *Briseadh agus brú ort!*'

Buinneach dhearg/bhuí ort
May you have red/yellow diarrhoea

[bwyn-yakh darig/bwee urt]

Bhí an tanc leathlán le peitreal inné agus anois níl faic fágtha ann. Buinneach dhearg ort!
There was half a tank of petrol in that car yesterday and now there's nothing in it. May you have red diarrhoea!

Having diarrhoea is bad, but red or yellow diarrhoea is catastrophic.

As a way of thanking you for getting this far in the book, I'm rewarding you with the beautiful word for 'diarrhoea' in Irish. It is better in Irish than any other language. *'Buinneach'* even sounds watery and spluttery when you say it. You seem to get away with things in an Irish kitchen when you tell your partner you've a 'touch of diarrhoea'. You could say you have an awful head cold or a sore throat or a migraine, and there would be no response. But saying you have diarrhoea? 'Oh God, was it bad? I'll get you the Imodium.' You get all the sympathy votes.

Having diarrhoea is bad, but red or yellow diarrhoea is catastrophic. You are not joking if you wish red diarrhoea on someone. It is the hot hole of fire, Mount Etna levels of the runs. Nothing but undeniable pain and discomfort, and it's never-ending. You would really have to dislike someone to say, *'Buinneach dhearg ort.'*

Fuckáil leat
Fuck you

[fuck-awl lat]

Chaith tú an samhradh i mBostún agus anois tá blas an Yank ort.
Arra, fuckáil leat, a mhac!
You spent the summer in Boston and now you're speaking like a Yank.
Arra, fuck you!

> *From the bars to the bogs, the mountains to the piers, the use of the word 'fuck' is widespread.*

There is a unique part of Connemara Gaeilge that has to do with the addition of *'-áil'* at the end of a word. The most common and, indeed, the most powerful example would be the ubiquitous *'fuckáil leat!'* From the bars to the bogs, the mountains to the piers, the use of the word 'fuck' is widespread. It's been adapted over the decades, and the addition of *'-áil'* at the end lends it a strong west of Ireland feel. Throwing in *'a mhac'* (my son/sunshine/my man) at the end gives it even more welly: *'Fuckáil leat, a mhac!'* 'Fuck you, sunshine.'

Irish people are masters of using the word 'fuck' in English. We can say it in a hundred different ways with different intonations, and it can mean all kinds of things: surprise, regret, irritation, joy. We can throw it into a conversation and there would be no hostility in it. It's part and parcel of our lives, so we've absorbed it into our native tongue with the simple addition of *'-áil'* at the end.

Mallacht Chromaill ort
The curse of Cromwell on you

[mawl-akht crum-all urt]

Mallacht Chromaill ort agus tú théis an bosca Trócaire a sciobadh.
The curse of Cromwell on you for robbing the Trócaire box.

> *You can practically hear the bailiffs knocking on the door, coming to take the cottage from you.*

Cromwell was a bad bastard, there are no two ways about it. He inflicted pain, punishment, and hardship on the Irish people for decades. He took away our land and gave it to the *Sasanaigh*. He sent tens of thousands of us on penal ships to the colonies of the British Empire. He attempted to eradicate the Irish people.

With that said, this insult needs very little explanation. It's an aul one from the dark times, when it was heard and used in villages all over Connemara by the local people. *'Mallacht Chromaill ort'* is heavy with centuries of persecution. You can practically hear the bailiffs knocking on the door, coming to take the cottage from you. I'm not pulling any punches with this one. I think I'd prefer someone to wish me *buinneach dhearg* (page 298) than say this to me.

Pian sa tóin (amach 's amach é)
Pain in the hole (without question)

[pee-an sa tone (amok s'amok ay)]

Ar chuala tú [INSERT NAME] *ar an raidió ar maidin? Pian sa tóin cheart é, ní raibh mé in ann éisteacht leis!*
Did you hear [INSERT NAME] on the radio this morning? A right pain in the hole, I couldn't listen to him!

Yer man in the open-plan office who says 'Half day?' when you try to leave work at ten to five.

'*Póg mo thóin*' is so '80s. I'm fed up with it. We've come a long way from there to here because Irish is more widespread. I can see it building and building, new words and old words mingling together. And so if you're going to use '*tóin*', make it a '*pian sa tóin*'. The word 'hole' brings more pain into it than 'ass'. Why dilute it? And if you add '*amach 's amach*' at the end of something, it means 'undoubtedly' or 'without question'.

Everyone reading this book will be able to think of someone they work with who is an utter *pian sa tóin*, whether it's in the teachers' break room, the aisles of a supermarket, the factory floor, or yer man in the open-plan office who says 'Half day?' when you try to leave work at ten to five. Next time you see them, just smile and think in your head, 'Do you know what you are? *Pian sa tóin amach 's amach thú.*'

NINE

Words for Ireland's uniquely unreliable weather

There's no better example of the unpredictability of the Irish weather than at the Galway Races. It's a microcosm for every type of weather event. Take your suncream and take your snorkel, because it might start out scorching with *an ghrian ag scoilteadh na gcloch* (page 312), but by the end it's like a zombie movie. The high heels are muddy and the fascinators are floppy. Even the cameraman is having difficulty following the horses because his lens is a shambles – you might see a tissue coming up to rub the drops of rain away when you're at home watching it on TV. A sure sign of proper Galway midsummer weather is when it's a complete mess at Ladies' Day, *tá sé ina phraiseach* (page 308).

The words in this chapter weren't made up by Met Éireann. You get the sense that they've been forged by our ancestors who worked outdoors for generations. We adore the weather, especially when we're moaning about it, and we're lucky that there are so many beautiful ways of talking about it in Irish. And, as a direct result of it raining out west 362 days of the year, most of the phrases describe shite weather. People toiling away outdoors led to a fertile environment for language, because you don't come up with great ways to talk about the cold or the heat from lying on your sofa looking out the window. These words come from being in the middle of it.

Tá sé ina phraiseach
It's a mess

[taw shay in-na frash-okh]

Bhí an lá ina phraiseach cheart nuair a bhíomar ag dreapadh Chruach Phádraig.
It was an awful day altogether the day we climbed Croagh Patrick.

It does no harm to you – as long as you have your expedition gear on.

I've been living in the west of Ireland for 25 years, and I've come to the conclusion that the rain that falls here is a type found nowhere else in the world. It sweeps in off the Atlantic Ocean and engulfs Galway almost every day of the year. To be in Galway in the high summer ... actually, no, that's the wrong term as it's never 'high summer' in Galway. To be in Galway in the middle of July and see the soft rain falling for most of the day is something to behold. Hour after hour of drizzle that hits you sideways. It does no harm to you – as long as you have your expedition gear on.

It always happens on those days when you try to get out for a walk. It could be beautiful when you set out to climb Croagh Patrick at 6 a.m., but by the time you get to the top, *tá sé ina phraiseach*. It's as if we take what the Atlantic gives us, the cloud breaks on the land and falls in the west, and they never get the half of it on the east of the country. Every time I go to Dublin it's dry, and every time I return to Galway, the minute I get over the bridge in Athlone, it starts raining again.

You can use *'ina phraiseach'* to describe a messy house as well. It's an all-rounder.

Ag stealladh báistí
Lashing down

[egg shtal-la bawsh-tee]

An nóiméad a d'fhág an fhoireann an seomra feistis thosaigh sé ag stealladh báistí.
The minute the team left the dressing room it started lashing down.

I've been in countries during rainy seasons and they're only in the halfpenny place in comparison to us.

We as a nation can relate to all levels of rainfall more than any other nation in the world. I've been in countries during rainy seasons and they're only in the halfpenny place in comparison to us. I've stood on the main streets of Dhaka in Bangladesh in 32-degree heat when the monsoon rains hit, and when it falls it falls fast and hard, but then it's gone.

Our rain is different. It lives with us in every single town, and it's always around the corner. If it's not here today it will definitely be here tomorrow. To top it off, we have developed colour-coding for our rainfall – orange, yellow and red – to describe how wet you'll get if you go outside without an umbrella. Even five-year-olds know it.

Driving in the rain isn't much better either. Cars in Ireland should have a special setting for windscreen wipers: slow, medium, fast, Irish. The wipers would be moving so fast trying to keep up with the lashings of rain that you wouldn't be able to see the road in front of you.

Tá an ghrian ag scoilteadh na gcloch
It's boiling out there

[taw on gree-an egg skwill-tcha na gluck]

Tá mé maraithe ag an teas, tá an ghrian ag scoilteadh na gcloch anseo!
I'm killed by the heat, it's really boiling out there!

*The seats burn the arse off you,
the steering wheel is sticky and
you could cook a fry on the dashboard.*

Everyone knows the true measure of how boiling it is is to get into the car with all the windows closed. You can almost taste the heat. The seats burn the arse off you, the steering wheel is sticky and you could cook a fry on the dashboard. We've a fixation with checking the temperature gauge in the car on a hot day so we can take a photo of it and send it to the WhatsApp groups: 'Jesus, would you look, it's 30 degrees in the car!' Then it gathers legs and by the afternoon someone has sent a photo showing 34 degrees. There's people all over the country in their Corsas and Corollas having a competition to see who's the most boiling.

'*Tá an ghrian ag scoilteadh na gcloch*' literally translates as 'the sun is splitting the stones'. It's the type of weather that we all want but we can't really deal with. It has the mammies of the country telling us to 'close the windows to keep the heat out'.

Tá sé meirbh
It's heavy out there

[taw shay meriv]

Tá tinneas cinn orm mar gheall go bhfuil sé chomh meirbh amuigh.
I have a headache because of how heavy the weather is.

> *If you were on the continent you'd say it's 'balmy', but because you're in Ireland it's 'muggy'.*

This is one for those close summer days, when the heat ripples off the tarmac and the smell of the freshly cut grass fills the air because all the dads in the neighbourhood have pulled out their lawnmowers. There's no sun but not much air either. If you were on the continent you'd say it's 'balmy', but because you're in Ireland it's 'muggy'. The fan is taken out of the attic and the Velux window that's been closed since 1995 is wrestled open. It's like Ireland turns into the Mediterranean, not a quilt in sight, and couples all over the country are turning to each other in bed saying, 'All we need these nights is sheets.'

It's the only time when Irish people are actually relieved to be naked, basking on their beds with the windows open all night hoping for even a hint of a breeze.

Tá sé gránna
It's ugly out there

[taw shay graw-na]

Níor theastaigh ó na gasúir dul amach sa gclós ag am lóin, bhí sé gránna amuigh.
The kids didn't want to go out into the yard on lunch break, it was an awful day out.

The squally days when the wind is up or when the hailstones are so big they nearly cut your skin.

The sound of *'gránna'* is bang-on to describe a horrible aul day of weather. It encapsulates those umpteen shite days every month that we endure, the squally days when the wind is up or when the hailstones are so big they nearly cut your skin. You'll know when it's truly *gránna* outside because you'll talk about it for five minutes non-stop as soon as you walk in the front door, and only then will you ask what's for dinner.

'*Gránna*' can be used to describe someone's physical appearance or character as well. It's a harsh word, and saying that about someone means they're almost witch-like evil. So best to stick to using it for the weather, for those nasty days when you wouldn't even put the dog out.

Tá an lá ina chac ceart
It's a real shite aul day

[taw on law inna cock kyart]

Idir thintreach agus toirneach, tá an lá ina chac ceart.
Between the thunder and lightning it's a shite aul day.

Can be used to say the weather is excrement levels of awful.

For those of you who want to know the Irish word for poo, it's *'cac'*. As well as the physical rubbish from the human body, *'cac'* can be used to say the weather is excrement levels of awful. Like everyone, I like knowing a few bold words in other languages, but the Spanish word for 'poo' landed me in *'cac'* in Bilbao in 1993.

I lived in a suburb called Algorta, and I was moving house so I wanted to get some boxes from the local supermarket to put my stuff into. There was a small shop beside my apartment block called Eroski, which is basically a Basque version of Dunnes Stores. Over the two years I'd been there, I got to know the people who worked at the checkouts: women in their fifties and sixties who were there every day when I went in to get my few bits. I was all good with *'buenos días'* and *'muchos gracias'*, but I had to Google the Spanish word for 'boxes'.

So I walked up to one of the women I thought I knew well, feeling cocky with my little bit of Spanish, and said, *'Hola, necesito dos cacas.'* And she looked stunned. Then the cashier behind her started laughing, the woman behind me in the queue started laughing, and then the whole place was in an uproar. And all I could say was *'Qué?'* Turns out 'boxes' in Spanish is *'cajas'*, not *'cacas'*, so I actually asked her for two shits.

So now you know, it's *'cac'* in Irish and *'caca'* in Spanish, but I doubt they have many shite aul days in Spain.

Tá sé marbh inniu
It's a humid dead aul day

[taw shay mar-iv inn-yu]

Oscail na fuinneoga! Scaoil isteach an t-aer.
Tá sé marbh inniu.
Open the windows! Let in some air.
It's a humid dead aul day.

The heat is hotter in Irish.

My favourite place to get the weather is TG4, no competition. RTÉ can keep their '70s global warming graphs; give me the modern map of Ireland on TG4 any day. All I want is a beautiful Connemara accent telling me it's *marbh inniu*. The presenters on TG4 have brought the weather to another level. They're so popular that a couple of the weather girls were even guests on the *Tommy Tiernan Show* and the nation fell in love with them. They know their Irish and by God do they know their weather.

They undoubtedly have far more ways of talking about the weather than I've included here, and *'tá sé marbh inniu'* probably isn't something they get to say often, but humidity takes on a whole new dimension when they do. The heat is hotter in Irish.

Tá scalach gaoithe ann
A strong breeze

[taw skawll-ock gwee aun]

Tá scalach gaoithe ag teacht isteach ón bhfarraige, lá maith le héadaí a thriomú!
There's a strong breeze coming in off the sea, it's a good day for drying the clothes!

> *I'd walk out of my little Sunsplash Cottage, look across the island and see the washing on the lines ferociously flapping in the wind.*

If there's a *scalach gaoithe* outside, you know it's a good day for drying. When you hit your forties, you get a great sense of achievement out of getting a few loads of clothes washed and dried in the one day. 'Jesus Christ, they're dry already! I'm going to do the sheets.' You get a thrill from taking the duvet off the bed that morning and putting it back on again that night. There's nothing that smells better than a quilt cover or a sheet that's been dried on the line. If you manage to get the towels done as well, then you have an honours degree in drying. As long as there's sunshine and a strong breeze, the smell of Irish wind mixed with Lenor will be wafting around the neighbourhood.

On Inis Meáin, when I'd walk out of my little Sunsplash Cottage and look across the island, I'd see the washing on the lines ferociously flapping in the wind, and I'd know that the *scalach gaoithe* inland would lift as soon as I got out on the open sea on the boat to the mainland. It might even be a *gála* (page 324).

Gála
Gale

[gaw-la]

Bhí gála ag séideadh i nGaillimh aréir. Bhí an trampoline *imithe ar maidin.*
There was a gale blowing in Galway last night. The trampoline was gone this morning.

> *There was no remedy for the way your brain and body felt in the motion of the boat navigating the swell of the grey, angry Atlantic.*

The *Rose of Aran* boat was my only connection to the mainland for nearly two years when I lived on Inis Meáin. The way the wind rose when the island disappeared in the distance and the waves grew angrier and higher was unforgettable. I learned pretty quickly out there about the wind and its power, the way the breeze could lift in minutes and change the complexion of the day. It was worse when the wind was strong and waves the size of houses would roll against the *Rose*, but somehow she would roll with them, the drumming hum of the diesel engine keeping her aligned and balanced.

There was no remedy for the way your brain and body felt in the motion of the boat navigating the swell of the grey, angry Atlantic in a *gála*. I always stood outside, my back tight against the iron stairwell, and focused on the horizon, taking in the air and moving with the flow, until the engines finally slowed, the breeze and water calmed down, and we reached land again.

Tá goimh ann
It's nippy cold

[taw gwiv aun]

Níl sé ag cur sneachta go fóill, ach tá goimh ann.
It's not snowing yet, but it's nippy out there.

It was −34 degrees Celsius, and for the next 40 days the only part of me visible was my eyes.

The nippiest I've ever been was in 2018, when I went to Siberia in winter to film the travel show. We flew from Dublin to Frankfurt to Moscow to Siberia, through four different time zones. The funny thing was that the Siberian air had travelled in the opposite direction to me, introducing itself to Ireland as the Beast from the East, but it seemed to get there much faster than the fourteen or so hours it took me to arrive in the remote outpost of Tomsk Oblast.

Winter starts in Siberia in September and sometimes doesn't finish until April or May. It was −34 degrees Celsius, and for the next 40 days the only part of me visible was my eyes. I had special merino wool liners underneath my big Arctic trousers, and base layers and secondary outer layers, but I could still only manage 30 minutes outside the Jeep. *Bhí goimh ann.* The land was completely permafrost, and the snowdrifts were 40 to 50 feet high. Yet life went on, and people could still go about their business, but when just a taste of Siberian weather landed in Ireland people were hoarding sliced pans and toilet rolls.

Tá bruith ann
It's boiling

[taw brih aun]

Cuir ort an t-uachtar gréine, tá bruith ann!
Get the sun cream on, it's boiling out there!

You land on the beach and you know within seconds that you're in the danger zone.

'*Tá bruith ann*' is for that Factor 50 weather. You land on the beach and you know within seconds that you're in the danger zone, but your cream gets all messed up in the sand and you end up applying a gritty paste to your boiling skin. At night in restaurants you can see the people who got caught out, shoulders and arms like embers and faces like pork crackling.

I'm an expert in getting burnt. If I don't apply suncream, I'll look like a sausage. I was burnt badly on a speedboat in Thailand when I was travelling to the island of Koh Pha-Ngan. It took me about five days of staying in the shade in the hotel to feel any relief. It was ridiculous and it was horrific. I ended up in a clinic when I arrived in Taiwan because the whole of my shoulders had turned into one giant blister. So if you find yourself saying '*Tá bruith ann*', you better have a bottle of water in one hand and a bottle of Soltan in the other.

Tá a theanga bheag amuigh ag an préachán
The crow is spitting out his tonsils

[taw a hawn-ga byug am-wih egg on pray-a-kawn]

Bhí sé os cionn 30 céim ar maidin, bhí a theanga bheag amuigh ag an préachán.
It was over 30 degrees today, the crow was spitting out his tonsils with the heat.

I've never seen a crow's tongue, but I'd imagine if he's spitting his tonsils out, he's unhappy.

This is another great one I got from Inis Meáin. Respect to the island elders who came up with this phrase. It literally means the crow's tongue is hanging out with the heat. I've never seen a crow's tongue, but I'd imagine if he's spitting his tonsils out, he's unhappy.

Maybe the crow went to Inis Meáin to escape Galway City in search of a better quality of life. He thought it would always be breezy, but a heatwave came in and he was trapped on the island until the next boat. Nothing to do but spit out his tonsils in fury. But he's an Irish-speaking crow, so he sticks it out because he's after getting a crow relocation grant from the government, which means he can move his mother and father and aunties and uncles and cousins to the island with him. And he reckons soon enough it'll be *ag stealladh báistí* (page 310) anyway.

So if you're on Inis Meáin, or any of the Aran Islands, and you hear a crow go *'Cá?'*, it might just be him.

Tháinig siota gaoithe
A breeze came

[haw-nig shut-a gwee-ha]

Chomh luath is a bhíomar ar an uisce tháinig siota gaoithe.
The minute we got out on the water, the breeze picked up.

All of a sudden the wind takes the sails, they unfurl and the boat glides along.

Inis Meáin is the land of weather. It's the first place the wind hits when it comes in from the west, so they have magical ways of describing it. These people are wind and water people, sailing people; the breeze means they can travel and fish. They have been in boats for centuries and they are reliant on the wind for power; there were no Yamaha or Suzuki engines back in the days of the currach.

You can imagine seeing a Galway Hooker out on the bay, languishing, then *tagann siota gaoithe isteach* and the sails go up. All of a sudden the wind takes the sails and they unfurl, and the boat glides along. When you depend on the sea for your livelihood and there's been a hot spell of weather where the days were flat, the breeze coming in can breathe life back into the island.

Tá sé gioblach
Rainy and windy/rough and ready

[taw shay gyub-al-ach]

Níor mhaith liom a bheith taobh amuigh agus an lá chomh gioblach sin.
That's not a day to be out, it's squally out there.

Tháinig sé ar ais ón bhféile cheoil agus cuma ghioblach go maith air.
He came back fairly dishevelled after the music festival.

> *That aul man who lives on his own*
> *at the bottom of the road,*
> *the bachelor who is a bit dishevelled.*

'*Tá sé gioblach*' is a phrase used in Ráth Chairn for rough weather and a rough-looking person. It describes that aul man who lives on his own at the bottom of the road, the bachelor who is a bit dishevelled. When it comes to weather, it's a great phrase for the unpredictable kind, when you have three seasons in one day.

I love when I see an Irish bullock or heifer standing there on its own in the middle of a field on a squally west of Ireland day. There's not one bit of shelter around. It's just the animal and the stone walls, and the rain lashing in sideways. And it doesn't seem to bother them. The weather might be *gioblach* but they look cool as anything. Connemara cattle are tough beasts. They know that, like most of the weather systems in the west, it will pass.

Aiteall
The gap between two showers

[at-ill]

Tá aiteall ann ... rith!
There's a break in the rain ... run!

When the clouds say, 'OK, let's take a break here for a minute.'

What a beautiful Irish word for a beautiful moment in Irish weather. This word is used in Ráth Chairn and Connemara, but it's a new word for me. An *aiteall* is the dry gap you get between two showers, when the clouds say, 'OK, let's take a break here for a minute.'

In Ireland, we live our lives in the *aiteall* – it's where we're most productive. In a word, it makes me think of that busy criss-crossing of Main Street you see when people are trying to get all their bits done. You might be sheltering in a shop doorway or under a big tree because you're wearing the wrong jacket, and you're waiting for a break in the rain so you can make a dash for it.

You could get hours of work done in a 10-minute *aiteall*; it has a way of focusing the mind. But the moment just before the *aiteall*, when we have to be still, could be used as a life lesson. You can take that time to be calm, have a break yourself before the clouds take their break, and know that in life, there's always going to be a gap between the showers.

Brádánach ceo
Wet, misty fog

[braw-dawn-ach key-oh]

D'éirigh mé ag a cúig a chlog ar maidin agus bhí brádánach ceo ann.
I got up at five this morning and there was a wet, misty fog out there.

When it's cold and there's no wind, the fog rolls down off the mountains, and the fog lights on the cars are switched on.

There are only a few times in our year of weather in Ireland that we need to turn on the fog lights. It's maybe twice a year, when it's cold and there's no wind, the fog rolls down off the mountains, and the fog lights on the cars are switched on. I love seeing fog. It feels like a special occasion, and I think everyone gets a small bit of pleasure from driving slowly in the *brádán* with all the eerie headlights coming towards you.

A popular word for 'fog' and 'mist' is *'ceo'*, and Ireland does a misty hill very well. Driving over the Conor Pass in Kerry on a misty morning is like something out of a Sherlock Holmes movie. You'd expect a nineteenth-century carriage to fly by. And you know Dingle is somewhere below, cosy under a blanket of *ceo*. I even love saying the word *'ceo'* – kyoooow – it has a lovely, simple sound.

Sioc
Frost

[shuck]

Bhí sioc géar ann aréir.
There was a hard frost last night.

> *I'd get up in my pyjamas and look out the window and everything would be white and frozen.*

When the grass makes that satisfying crunch underneath your feet, you know it's *sioc*. I used to wake up in Navan in the mornings when I was a kid and my mam or dad would tell me, 'Ohh, there was a hard frost last night,' and I'd get up in my pyjamas and look out the window and everything would be white and frozen. Jack Frost had been out and about. I'd look out the kitchen window and the basin that was always outside on the step had frozen water in it. Then the call would come from the school: 'Pipes are burst. No school today.' It's one of the greatest gifts any child can get. And my dad would be running hot water through the system in a panic. When we used to go on holidays in the '70s, my dad would leave the hot water tap dripping to stop the pipes from freezing just in case there was a cold snap while we were away. Frozen pipes in Ireland are a natural disaster, unless you're a schoolchild who can spend the day exploring the fields covered in *sioc* instead of going to school.

Sioc go gaineamh rua
Hard frost

[shuck guh gon-yiv roo-a]

Bhí sioc go gaineamh rua ar maidin i gCois Fharraige ag a seacht a chlog ar maidin.
There was a really hard frost in Cois Fharraige at seven o'clock this morning.

> *There's nothing like your mother running out of the house in 1981 in her dressing gown with a saucepan of lukewarm water to melt the ice on the car windscreen.*

This phrase for hard frost was given to me by Aoife Ní Thuairisg, one of the original weather presenters on TG4. It's a phrase spoken by the people of Cois Fharraige, who live on the coastal side of Connemara. It means 'a frost so hard it will go deep into the red sand'. It makes sense that a beautifully descriptive phrase like this would be used by beach people, where in bad weather the hard frost might meet the golden sands of the coast.

It's a perfect phrase to describe that really bad frost we get in Ireland a few times a year, and when that frost hits, it always hits the midlands harder than the coast. I grew up in Navan with the Great Saucepan Tradition every time a hard frost hit. There's nothing like your mother running out of the house in 1981 in her dressing gown with a saucepan of lukewarm water to melt the ice on the car windscreen.

I've carried on that tradition now with my family, and I know if I see the saucepan on the front step that there was frost when my wife was leaving for work at seven that morning. And if it's a *sioc go gaineamh rua*, hours later I'll still have to take the saucepan back inside and refill it with lukewarm water to clear the windscreen. My two young lads know all about the Great Saucepan Tradition now too, so it will be passed on to the next generation.

Léasán/bogha báistí/tuar ceatha
Rainbow

[lays-awn / bow-ah bawsh-tee / tu-ar kyah-ha]

Bhí bogha báistí álainn thar Chnoc Meá an tráthnóna samhradh sin.
There was a lovely rainbow over Knockmaa that summer afternoon.

Cityscape, countryside, on the M50 or in your back garden, rainbows don't partake in geographical discrimination.

These are three beautiful words to describe an amazing thing that happens over the fields of Ireland. Cityscape, countryside, on the M50 or in your back garden, rainbows don't partake in geographical discrimination. We should never take a rainbow for granted because they're magical, and that's reflected in the fact that there are three different ways to say 'rainbow' in Irish.

We have the best rainbows in the world, and I'm not interested in a scientific expert telling me how they happen. I want to believe that fairies are in charge of rainbows. That Ériu, goddess of Ireland, is telling her land spirits, 'Throw a rainbow at the back of Lackagh at about quarter past twelve and leave it up for about nine minutes, will ya? And there's a wedding in the Skellig Hotel in Dingle at four o'clock so give them all the colours and make sure it's a big one.' And she's doing it to see who has their eyes open to it, that these *boghanna báistí* aren't made by a special effects company in Kilkenny or somewhere, they're out of our hands. So we need to stop, get the family out of the car, and take five minutes to appreciate these wonders of the world.

TEN

The *cúpla focal* for going about your day

The Irish language is changing all the time. I went to college to do Early and Modern Irish in 1986, but 'modern' Irish now is different to the 'modern' Irish I was studying then. It has grown and adapted to our environment.

The Concise English–Irish Dictionary by Pádraig Ó Mianáin was published in 2020, and it was the first new Irish dictionary to be compiled in over 60 years. The thousands of modern Irish phrases it lists shows that the language was anything but stagnant over those decades – it was flourishing. Irish has changed, and it is going to keep changing, because people speak it daily in all kinds of situations. There are friends living together in flats or meeting up in pubs or going to festivals who are speaking Irish. It doesn't just exist in the classroom.

I could have chosen hundreds of phrases for this chapter, but I chose words that popped into my head as I was going about my day. It is like a bowl of Gaeilge potpourri. A few of the words are fairly new to the Irish language. They definitely wouldn't have been around in the days of the lads getting off the currach with the keg of Guinness, and it's probably the only chapter in the book that might be able to teach the great Irish-speakers of Connemara a new word. Other words are for things you see so often that you probably don't give them a second thought, like beans and screwdrivers and rusty gates. I like to think the words you're about to read show how flexible Irish is, that it is a language of the present, not of the past.

Ócáid
Gathering/event

[oh-cawj]

Tá ócáid ar siúl ar an Domhnach, tá an chlann ar fad ag dul ann.
There's a get-together on Sunday, all the family are going.

The house was rammed with cousins and the kitchen never stopped: egg salad sambos, tea, apple tart, tea, pavlova, tea, more sambos, more tea ...

'Ócáid' is a word you can use if you're having a family gathering, like a twenty-first or a fiftieth wedding anniversary, where every aunt, uncle, cousin and second cousin turns up at the house for a celebration.

We had an *ócáid* in my Aunty Ray's house every Saturday when I was a child. We would go to Oliver Plunkett's Church for mass at seven. St Mary's was our closest church, but Mam thought Saturday night mass called for an excursion to the top of the town. Oliver Plunkett's was like one of those new builds you see on *Grand Designs*. It was a modern church with tasteful carpets, exposed beams, and minimalist Stations of the Cross. It even had a band with a drummer and a bass guitar, which I thought was revolutionary. The hymns sounded like funky bass tunes.

After mass, we would go to Aunty Ray's. It was an unofficial family gathering every Saturday night. The house was rammed with cousins and the kitchen never stopped: egg salad sambos, tea, apple tart, tea, pavlova, tea, more sambos, more tea ... Aunty Ray lived in a big farmhouse and the door was always swung open, with wellies and walking boots lining the hallway, and a smell of cow dung outside. My mother loved going there for an *ócáid*, so I want to give a shout-out to her and my two wonderful aunties who have passed away, Aunty Breda and Aunty Ray, and Mammy Tríona. You made our Saturday nights.

Mamó
Gran/Nana

[mam-oh]

Beidh Mamó ag teacht don Nollaig.
Mamó will be here for Christmas.

> *She taught me to drink tea at the tender age of seven.*

In Irish, you wouldn't really call your granny *'seanmháthair'*, just as you wouldn't really call her 'grandmother' in English. *'Mamó'* is an endearing family term, just like saying 'Nana', 'Nanny', or 'Gran' in English.

My *mamó* on my mother's side, Nana Larkin, used to ride a High Nelly bicycle around Curraghaun in Tuam. She'd cycle around the townland and stop by people's houses so they could swap stories and sing songs and have a little *scealpóg fuisce* (page 182). I never met her, but I can feel her DNA in me. I'm living about 15 miles from Tuam and I feel as if I was drawn to Galway because of her.

My other mamó, Nana Keogan, used to drive a red Mini around Navan. She must have looked so stylish zipping around the town. I learned a lesson from her that I've kept with me all my life: how to drink tea. She taught me to drink tea at the tender age of seven. She saw that I had a taste for it and she encouraged it. Now making a cup of tea is a process of divine inspiration for me. My eldest son seems to have inherited my *grá* for *tae*, but he only drinks it when he gets home from college on a Friday at about eight o'clock in the evening, and I'm the only one who can make it right for him. Never underestimate the power of putting on the kettle; it is a spiritual moment between two people.

Daideo
Granda/Pops

[dad-oh]

Thaitin Páirc an Chrócaigh go mór le Daideo.
Daideo loved going to Croke Park.

> *Between Daideo Keogan on my dad's side and Daideo Larkin on my mam's, the four pillars of my family were GAA, farming, pints and drapery.*

As with *'mamó'* (page 350), *'daideo'* is an affectionate term for 'grandfather' in Irish. My father's father, Granda Keogan, was one of the first men in Navan to buy a car. He was an entrepreneur so the Keogans were doing OK back in the 1950s. He ran a shop called Keogan and Carty, which was on Main Street for thirty-something years. My father went to London to study tailoring with Moss Bros., and eventually took over the shop. Between them, I'd say they put suits on thousands of Navan men, and on young Navan boys making their first holy communions and confirmations.

The shop was in the shadow of St Mary's Church, so there was always lots of foot traffic, and I remember standing in the shop listening to all the stories while my dad cut yards of fabric so women could get new curtains made. Between Daideo Keogan on my dad's side and Daideo Larkin on my mam's, the four pillars of my family were GAA, farming, pints, and drapery. I've managed to continue two of them.

Ainm baile
Home name

[an-im bal-ya]

Cé thusa?
Sonny Choilm Learaí is ainm baile dom.
Who are you?
Sonny Colm Larry is my home name.

One of the ways the locals can really get to grips with who you are is by knowing who your parents and grandparents and great-grandparents are.

The way they use family names in Connemara is tribal. An *'ainm baile'* combines your name with your ancestors' names to distinguish who you are and which lineage you belong to. It's ancient Irish clan stuff that goes back centuries, but some still use it today in certain enclaves in Connemara.

Southern and western Connemara can only be accessed by bridge – it's known locally as *'na hoileáin'*, 'the islands' – and one of the ways the locals can really get to grips with who you are is by knowing who your parents and grandparents and great-grandparents are. If you are in your mother's area, you would use her lineage, but if you're in your father's, you use his. So Edel would come home after living in London for a few years and say she's Edel Bhriain Mháirtín Shéamuis – her name, her father's name, her grandfather's name, and her great-grandfather's name. I think it's brilliant. But, before you start giving yourself an *ainm baile*, you can't use this if you're from Meath or Mayo or Dublin; it's unique to a small part of Connemara.

Gabh i leith (goile)
Come over here to me now (c'mere)

[gull-ya]

Goile anseo go Mamaí.
Come over here to Mammy.

Can be used if you're leaning out the window of the car asking for directions, or if you're a GAA coach beckoning over a 10-year-old player.

This is brilliant Connemara Irish, and all I want to do is get it out there in Ireland and have loads of people saying it. It means 'Come into my presence'. *'Gabh i leith'* is how you spell it, but the way you say it has been sculpted and moulded over decades of use by Irish-speakers, so it has to be condensed to *'goile'* (gull-ya) to sound right. It's a friendly, casual phrase that can be used if you're leaning out the window of the car asking for directions, or if you're a GAA coach beckoning over a 10-year-old player: 'C'mere for a second, Aisling.' It's an endearing phrase that expresses closeness. You might see a child fall in a playground and hurt their little knee, and their mammy or daddy would say to them, *'Goile anseo.* Are you alright?' It's almost impossible to say *'goile'* without a physical gesture. You have to lean in, open your arms, or give the curly finger.

Bísire
Screwdriver

[bee-sha-ra]

Ba chóir go mbeadh réimse maith bísirí i ngach teach in Éireann.
Every house in Ireland should have a decent range of screwdrivers.

I have a serious selection of Phillips and flatheads that I've built up over the years.

I learned this word from Fiona Ní Chléirigh, the principal of the Gaeltacht college I went to in St Mel's in Longford as a teenager. She was a cool principal and she had a huge influence on me as a 15- or 16-year-old prefect. She knew I liked to learn new words, so she taught me *'bísire'*, even though it would be a few years before I would have one of my own.

Now I have a serious selection of Phillips and flatheads that I've built up over the years. I have miniature ones in The Drawer of Shite Bits in the kitchen and heavy-duty ones in the shed. I got myself a toolbox for my screwdrivers and other bits, and now I feel complete.

You might think there's nothing more unglamorous than a screwdriver, but I think they should be given more praise. I love seeing lads hop out of a van wearing their Snickers work trousers with their collection of multicoloured screwdrivers in the pockets. To me, those lads are like gun-slingers in the Wild West. They're ready to rewire your house or fix your skirting boards but they wouldn't be able to do it without the humble *bísire*.

Cadhnra
Battery

[kai-na-ra]

D'imigh an leictreachas aréir sa stoirm, buíochas le Dia bhí cadhnra sa torch mór dearg a bhí sa chófra.
The electricity went last night in the storm, thank God there was a battery in the big red torch in the press.

Think about all the High Nellys with their dynamo lights, the Honda 50s used to get from A to B, and massive torches for walking down dark roads.

Along with *'bísire'* (page 358), *'cadhnra'* is another word I learned from Fiona Ní Chléirigh. It is a modern word that has emerged as technology has changed. Even when they had batteries in Connemara and the Aran Islands way back in the day, they wouldn't have had an Irish word for it. If you think about all the High Nellys with their dynamo lights, the Honda 50s used to get from A to B, and massive torches for walking down dark roads, there must have been thousands of *cadhnraí* in the west of Ireland.

Even so, people from Connemara would prefer to take the English word and make it sound Irish, and add a 'h' when it's *their* battery: 'mo bhattery', pronounced 'watt-ery'. I've heard people in the west going about their lives say, *'Cá bhfuil mo bhicycle?'* when every child in primary school learns that the Irish word for 'bicycle' is *'rothar'*. People just don't use *'rothar'*, preferring to pronounce it 'why-cicle'.

'Cadhnra' is a useful everyday word for a useful everyday item, and this might be a new word for native Irish-speakers in the west of Ireland. Ironically, though, it's probably more natural and fluent to say 'mo bhattery'.

Gríscíní uaineola
Lamb chops

[gris-key-nee oo-an yo-la]

Is breá linn ar fad gríscíní uaineola le prátaí i mo theach.
We all love lamb chops with spuds in our house.

> *When it's a Tuesday afternoon in the middle of July, and out comes a massive plate of lamb chops, you have to have the language to teach them.*

When I went to Coláiste na bhFiann as a *cúntóir* (prefect) when I was 16, I was in charge of a group of about ten kids. From the beginning of the three weeks that they would be in the Gaeltacht, they were my little family. I had to make sure that they were alright. I had to make sure that they were happy. I had to make sure that they were eating. I would help them out with the necessary nouns and verbs to get through the day. And what better way to learn a language than sitting around a table at dinner? So when it's a Tuesday afternoon in the middle of July, and out comes a massive plate of lamb chops, you have to have the language to teach them.

And so I had the pleasure of passing on the word for 'chops' in Irish: '*gríscíní*'. It even sounds meaty. So at eight and nine years of age, these kids have the Irish language bubbling away under the surface, and they'll remember the word for chops because they'll remember the taste – and the only way to eat *gríscíní uaineola* is to pick them up and attack them with your teeth.

Sceallóga
Chips

[ska-low-ga]

Bhí snack box *agam aréir, agus bhí na sceallóga go hálainn.*
I had a snack box last night, and the chips were lovely.

> *I can't think of a place
> more magical than a chipper.*

'*Scealloga*' is one of the greatest words I know in the Irish language, and it's the word for chips. There are many magical words in this book, but I can't think of a place more magical than a chipper. I am a chipper man, through and through, and I like to have chips every Friday for dinner. It's religion.

Years and years ago, the RTÉ show *Nationwide* did a special on me where I went back to visit my hometown of Navan, so I brought them to all the hot spots, which naturally included my favourite chipper, Ezio's. Every time I go back home, I bring my boys in for fish and chips. I'm proud that the only depiction of me in Navan isn't in the town hall or my local school, it's in my favourite chipper. It's a cut-out from an article in the *Meath Chronicle* about the *Nationwide* special with the title 'Home is the Hero'. That's how seriously I love my *scealloga*.

Pónairí
Beans

[poh-neh-ree]

D'ith mé pónairí gach lá ar an ollscoil i mBaile Átha Cliath.
I ate beans every day in college in Dublin.

*Dympna has reintroduced them to the
Ó hEochagáin household,
and it's reignited my taste for them.*

I abandoned Batchelors and left baked beans in my past for years. I don't know if it's because I ate too many of them in the '80s or if I just went off them. Dympna has reintroduced them to the Ó hEochagáin household, and it's reignited my taste for them. Now every Saturday morning is bean time. We always have a big grill, with sausages, bacon, black and white pudding ... but the plate isn't fully dressed unless you finish it off with a few spoonfuls of beans.

'*Pónairí*' can be used for any kind of beans, but there's only one type of bean in Ireland that matters and that's baked beans. Learning this word when I was a child in the Gaeltacht changed my view of the language – it made it less alien to know there was a word for such a simple thing. And we all know the rhyme: 'Beans, beans are good for your heart, the more you eat, the more you ...' '*Pónairí*' even sounds like it's going to make you fart.

Builín
A loaf

[bwill-een]

Cheannaigh mé builín batch úr álainn ar maidin, ar mhaith leat slisín tósta?
I bought a lovely fresh batch loaf this morning, do you fancy a slice toasted?

> *My dad would cut massive slices with a bread knife, and we'd have to put them under the grill to toast them because they were too thick for the toaster.*

When I was a young lad, there was a bakery in town called Spicers and they made the best bread in Navan. Their tagline was 'Spicers are nicer', and they were right. They had red and white plastic packaging and you would know it anywhere. They would send platoons of batch bread out into the town, and we would always buy one on a Friday or a Saturday morning. My dad would cut massive slices with a bread knife, and we'd have to put them under the grill to toast them because they were too thick for the toaster. You'd need copious amounts of butter to seep into the bread. I can still taste it.

'*Builín*' is a brilliant Irish word for 'loaf'. When I say it, I can see that perfect shape of batch bread, with the soft sides and the lovely brown, crusty top. A freshly baked *builín aráin* (loaf of bread) is a piece of art.

Taise
Dampness

[tash]

Tá spota taise ollmhór ar an tsíleáil os cionn an fholctha thuas staighre.
There's a huge damp spot on the ceiling above the bath upstairs.

> *You go into the shower and there's a fungus growing out of the roof like mushrooms.*

I don't know how we survived living in those bungalows we built in rural Ireland in the '60s and '70s, because we might have been good at building bungalows, but we weren't good at insulating them. I wouldn't go as far as saying our bungalow was damp, but let's just say it wasn't warm.

I remember getting up for school and putting on my clothes, and there would be a hint of dampness off them. There's nothing more educational than getting up in an Irish house in the '70s and the house is freezing. You go into the shower and there's a fungus growing out of the roof like mushrooms. But nobody cared. You just got on with it. Dampness was part of life in Ireland back then. It's not like today when we can turn on the underfloor heating, fire up the wood-chip boiler and wait for the geothermal air pump to kick in.

'Did you pump the walls?'
'Yeah, yeah, yeah. I got the walls pumped.'
'Did you get the beads in?'
'Yeah, yeah, yeah. I did, mate. Not a crack that hasn't been sealed.'

We've turned ourselves into insulation, we've made ourselves soft. When I was growing up, we had one electric blanket in the house and it didn't even cover the length of the bed. We used to steal the tiny square off my mam's bed and turn it up to three. Now our houses are like big electric blankets. Not a sign of *taise*.

Meirgeach
Rusty

[mer-rig-och]

Ghearr mé mo lámh ar an ngeata meirgeach, bhí orm shot *a fháil ón dochtúir.*
I cut my hand on the rusty gate, had to get a shot off the doctor.

> *Rust grows on things that have stood the test of time, like an old padlock on a garden shed or your childhood bicycle.*

When I was a child, I was worried about cutting myself on a rusty gate and needing a tetanus injection. My dad was always warning us about rusty gates, because rust is part of country life. There's the rusty farm machinery, the rusty nail, rusty barbed wire. But we'd climb over the gates anyway because that's how you got around, and we all ended up cutting ourselves and having to get tetanus injections.

So *meirgeach* meant 'danger' to me as a kid, but now I think there's something lovely about rust. It brings up feelings of nostalgia. Rust grows on things that have stood the test of time, like an old padlock on a garden shed or your childhood bicycle. Now I warn my boys about rusty gates, but they've climbed over them anyway, cut themselves, and ended up having to get tetanus injections.

Puiteach
Muck

[pwit-tchokh]

Dá bhfeicfá an phuiteach a bhí ag an Ploughing an tseachtain seo caite, linn snámha de phuiteach a bhí ann. If you saw the muck that was at the Ploughing last week, it was like a swimming pool of mud.

> *The great byproduct of our great Irish climate – 'mud' is American but 'muck' is Irish.*

I love the smell of muck; it's the smell of earth, and earth is a great thing. I've been to countries that have so little rain that they don't really have muck. It's the great byproduct of our great Irish climate – 'mud' is American but 'muck' is Irish.

I love seeing those photos of jockeys after a race, their faces covered in muck. They've gone through about three pairs of goggles during the race and you know the going was heavy because their heads look like Jackson Pollock paintings. People worry about standing in muck or a child getting mucky, but there's no harm in it. There's really nothing bad in muck at all.

'*Puiteach*' can be used only for 'soil', and you can't use it as an adjective to describe a meal or a football match. We should give our *puiteach* more praise because it's the most fertile muck in the world. If there's no muck, there's no farmers, and if there's no farmers, there's no food. Muck is life.

Bunoscionn
Upside-down

[bun-ows kyown]

Tá na cuairteoirí ag teacht ar an Aoine, agus tá an teach bunoscionn.
The visitors are coming Friday and the house is upside-down.

> *The fun of the word disappears when you become an adult; you never want to be upside-down, unless you're doing yoga.*

The literal translation of *'bunoscionn'* is 'bottom-side up', which makes me think of that lovely moment a mammy or daddy turns their toddler upside-down and the child is just loving it. It's such an alive and playful word, even in English. Kids always want to be *bunoscionn*, so they tumble down hills and do handstands.

We used to call rolling down a hill 'tumble the hog' when I was growing up, but when's the last time an adult ever had a good tumble the hog? The fun of the word disappears when you become an adult; you never want to be upside-down, unless you're doing yoga. You say your house is upside-down if it's messy, or that your life is upside-down if you're stressed. It's an everyday word that changes meaning the older you get, but we need to bring back the fun of *bunoscionn*.

Tada/faic
Nothing

[taw-da/fwak]

*Is breá liom an Satharn, ag luí ar an g*couch, *faic le déanamh ach breathnú ar an spórt.*
I love a Saturday with nothing on, lying on the couch watching sport.

> *It's a useful one when your son or daughter is supposed to be studying for the Leaving Cert, but they haven't done a tap.*

You have nothing planned. You're not going to talk to anyone. You're not going to do anything. Even if the postman comes to the door, you couldn't be bothered getting off the sofa. *'Tada'* and *'faic'* are two ways to say 'nothing' in Irish, for when you are having a day off. 'Are you up to anything today?' *'Tada.'*

These words are interchangeable – there's very little difference in their usage – but I am fond of the pronunciation of *'faic'*: 'fwak', as in 'whack' with an 'f' in front of it. I can feel the nothingness echoing off it. It's a useful one when your son or daughter is supposed to be studying for the Leaving Cert, but they haven't done a tap. 'My Miriam is studying day and night, so she is. Has your Caitríona been doing much?', and your only response can be an honest one: *'Faic*-all.'

Réasúnta
Grand/middling

[ray-zoon-ta]

Bhí me sna Canaries an tseachtain seo caite.
Conas a bhí an aimsir?
Bhí sé réasúnta, ní raibh sé iontach te.
I was in the Canaries last week.
What was the weather like?
It was only middling, it wasn't that hot.

> *The way Irish people use 'grand' is a masterclass in itself.*

'*Réasúnta*' is a word to describe how you're doing in your mind and in your body. When you're not feeling 100 per cent, but you don't know where to start. 'How did the exam go?' 'Middling ... grand.' You did okay, but you could have done better. 'How are you doing after the injury?' 'Grand.' You're feeling OK, but you could feel better.

The way Irish people use 'grand' is a masterclass in itself. It means multitudes and absolutely nothing at the same time. It is a perfect response when you want to leave the conversation open, to let people know that you're not bad but you're not good either, so there's more to be said. If you say you're '*réasúnta*' to someone you know well, they'll ask you what's wrong, what happened, is all OK? It's a simple way of describing a complicated state of being.

Dair ghaelach
Oak tree

[dar gway-lock]

Tháinig na Vikings *go hÉirinn fadó ag cuardach na darach gaelaí le haghaidh na long mór a bhí acu.*
The Vikings came here a long time ago in search of Irish oak for their longboats.

> *When Ireland was a big massive forest of oak, a squirrel could go from Malin Head to Mizen Head and never touch the ground.*

In Ireland, when we move into a house, we always plant a laurel hedge in the garden. It's the great hedge of Ireland. 'And did you get the laurel hedge in?' 'Yeah. Lovely green laurel hedge.' Ireland is full of fucking laurel hedges, up and down the country, and they're the most boring thing you can put in your garden. When we moved into our house, I wanted to make my garden different, so I decided to plant trees. I planted mountain ash, beech, silver birch, and I planted an oak tree. There's a myth that when Ireland was a big massive forest of oak, a squirrel could go from Malin Head to Mizen Head and never touch the ground. I don't think he would have made it if Ireland was full of laurel hedges.

The oak is one of Ireland's great indigenous trees. Oaks are full of our Celtic blood. *'Dair ghaelach'* even sounds like the name of an old Irish god. Vikings came here for our oak so they could make their longboats. That's how amazing our Irish oaks were – and of course we cut them all down. So if you're moving into a new house and you have the space in your garden, plant trees if you can. And if you plant a *dair ghaelach*, you'll know you're putting down strong roots.

ELEVEN

Lucky dip

Welcome to the odds and ends – more great words I love to use that didn't really fit anywhere else. It's a lost and found box of a chapter, but putting them here doesn't mean they're any less special or interesting. You could take a lucky dip and come out with anything. You could be trying to get concert tickets but there's *an-tóir* on them (big demand, page 402), or maybe you're relaxing with friends after a long week so you smoke some *raithneach* (weed, page 394).

'Miscellaneous' itself is a strange word. I have a folder on my laptop called 'Misc' and I don't really know what's in it. I probably only say the word once a year when I'm talking to my accountant: 'Oh yeah, just put that down under miscellaneous.' And this chapter is similar – the words are uncategorisable. 'Miscellaneous' doesn't have a direct translation in Irish. I had to look it up because there are even miscellaneous ways to say 'miscellaneous' *as Gaeilge*. It's *'éagsúil'* if you're talking about a collection of things or people and *'ilchineálach'* if you're talking about a collection of letters. So I've gone with *'meascra'*, which is used for a 'miscellany' of items in a book.

I think we're a jumble of things in Ireland anyway: our weather is 'mixed', an Irish stew is a little bit of this and a little bit of that, and we have a mishmash of accents for such a small island. So you'll find words here for any situation you find yourself in, even if you're trying to smuggle (*caimiléireacht*, page 396) teabags over to your sister in Australia.

Loinnir
Glistening/Feeling of merriness after early pints

[lyun-ar]

Bhí pionta agam ar maidin Tigh Ned in Inis Oirr, tháining mé amach agus bhí loinnir álainn ón uisce ag breathnú amach go hInis Meáin.
I had a morning pint in Tigh Ned in Inis Oírr, and when I came out the water had a beautiful glistening on it looking out to Inis Meáin.

> *You walk onto the beach and you see the sunshine almost dancing on top of the beautiful blue Atlantic waves.*

I get asked about this word at least once a week. When myself, Tommy and Laurita recorded the *Three Pints Please* podcast, I almost always spoke about feeling *'loinnir'*, and there would inevitably be a message from a listener a few days later asking me about it. It is a unique Irish word used to describe that merry feeling you get after having one or two pints early in the day. But it has to be before midday and it can be no more than two pints – instead of micro-dosing, it's porter-dosing.

The word *'loinnir'* also describes the sun glistening on the water, so its original meaning is lovely in its own right. You walk onto the beach and you see the sunshine almost dancing on top of the beautiful blue Atlantic waves. In fact, I first learned the word from a listener of the podcast called Patrick (@IHaveATribe) who messaged us on X to tell us about the *loinnir* on Inis Oírr. And a man from Wexford told me only recently that he uses it to describe the shine on freshly ploughed soil.

But the word has grown legs and Irish-speakers have adapted it to describe a similar experience: a glistening feeling in your head after a couple of pints, most likely at 9 a.m. in the airport while you're waiting for your flight.

Fite fuaite
Engrained/woven

[fih-tcha foo-ih-tcha]

Tá na ballaí clocha fite fuaite timpeall an chontae ar fad thiar i nGaillimh.
The stone walls are engrained on the land all over County Galway.

> *The Tara Mines near Navan, with their deep tunnels sprawling out for miles and miles under Meath.*

When I say 'fite fuaite', I can see the needle puncturing the cloth, the mammy sewing a button on a shirt, ink being tattooed onto skin. The roots of trees are woven into the soil, reaching down through the ground. It describes the Tara Mines near Navan, with their deep tunnels sprawling out for miles and miles under Meath. You could say that in Kerry, Gaelic football is *fite fuaite* in every single person in the county.

'*Fite fuaite*' is one of the nicest phrases I've learned in Irish, and saying it makes me happy: 'fih-cha foo-ih-cha'. It's like a little rhyme. Everything that's *fite fuaite* means it's engrained in your mind, in your body, in your soul, and in the landscape. It's absolutely part of everything you do. It's a phrase to be taken out on special occasions. It is the initials etched into a tree with a penknife to declare your love.

Plódaithe
Rammed/packed

[ploh-da-ha]

Bhí an chraic go maith síos sa local aréir, bhí an áit plódaithe.
The *craic* was good last night in the local, it was packed.

High summer drinks, friends meeting on Christmas Eve, or Stephen's Day when the races are on and the place is heaving.

This word has to have originated in small, old-style pubs when the queue at the bar is six people. It's for high summer drinks, friends meeting on Christmas Eve, or Stephen's Day when the races are on and the place is heaving – when everyone had the same idea and it was to go to the pub. I want to give a shout-out to five great pubs in Ireland that are always *plódaithe*:

Henry Loughran's in Navan
The Stag's Head in Dublin
Bob Griffin's Bar in Dingle
The Summerfield in Claregalway
Reapy's in Tuam

This word is used for events, not for the barbecue you had out the back in July. It's a perfect way to describe Diamond's Nightclub in the Ardboyne Hotel in 1987. It was the place to be on New Year's Eve in Navan. My mam would drop us off outside the nightclub at eight o'clock in the evening and we would have to queue for hours to get in for those few seconds of a countdown at midnight. Then the next day, Mam would ask the question we all love asking as parents when the teenagers have been out the night before: 'Well, was there a great crowd there?' And there always was. *Bhí sé plódaithe.*

Sáite
Stuck

[saw-tcha]

Bhí mé sáite sa leabhar seo le dhá bhliain anuas.
I was stuck into this book over the last two years.

You'd be watching a children's movie and inevitably someone would get stuck in quicksand.

'*Sáite*' has connotations of being stuck in quicksand. For some reason this was one of the greatest childhood fears in '80s and '90s Ireland. You'd be watching a children's movie and inevitably someone would get stuck in quicksand. There should have been quicksand classes to teach the children of Ireland how to get out of it if they found themselves stuck, even though I doubt there's a patch of quicksand in the country. Ray Mears would know what to do. We should get him over to run special bushcraft courses for 11-year-olds. I'd trust Ray Mears over Bear Grylls any day, especially when it comes to quicksand – it's a case of premier league versus the fourth division.

'*Sáite*' can also mean to be really deep into something, like your thesis or a project at work or an artist making a sculpture. You have to keep the head down because whatever it is, you're *sáite* until the deadline. It is a word you can use for being stuck in your work or stuck in quicksand – though in Ireland it's more likely to be muck (page 374).

Raithneach
Weed/ganja (seaweed)

[ran-ock]

Tá úsáid raithní dleathach anois in an-chuid tíortha ar domhan.
The use of ganja is becoming legal in many countries worldwide.

> *When you're hundreds of miles off the coast of Ireland, you might fancy a few puffs of a joint after a hard day's work at sea.*

I see no danger in anything that grows out of the ground, and I think there is a lack of understanding about marijuana in this country. When I was in California to film the travel show, I got to visit some of the weed dispensaries they have there. It was like walking into Holland & Barrett. They have baristas for the weed called 'budologists' who make sure you're getting the right type and the right dosage. Then I was able to visit a place in the Coachella Valley called Hot Springs where they have massive grow houses the size of IKEA. I had to get showered down and disinfected and put on all the white gear just to go inside. It's a scientific, controlled environment, like the Glanbia of ganja.

If you're out with a friend, you don't say, 'Have you got any marijuana there?' You say 'weed' or 'hash' or 'ganja'. *'Raithneach'* is an Irish word for 'seaweed', and it's been adopted as a slang term for hash. I imagine it was fishermen working long days out in Porcupine Banks who came up with it, because when you're hundreds of miles off the coast of Ireland, you might fancy a few puffs of a joint after a hard day's work at sea. I think we should be giving them credit for coming up with a great Irish slang word by using *'raithneach'* instead of 'hash' from English.

Caimiléireacht
Smuggling

[kam-a-ler-okht]

Bhí caimiléireacht ar siúl thar an teorainn le fada an lá.
Smuggling has been happening across the border for many years.

Irish people smuggle Barry's teabags and coleslaw and brown bread onto the Costa del Sol every year.

Growing up in Navan, you're only 40 miles from the border, so you know all about smuggling. Dundalk is just over the road and it's the great Cash & Carry of smuggling on the Silk Road from Belfast to Dublin. It was like the Khyber Pass between Afghanistan and Pakistan. Then I read about the smuggler Mr Nice. He wondered where the easiest place to smuggle hash would be and he chose Shannon Airport. I have this image in my head of a fleet of Volvo 740s with boots full of hash in long-term parking and no one having a clue.

He was one of the first big smugglers I heard of, but Ireland has a long tradition of smuggling going back centuries. The *poitín* makers in Connemara became experts at smuggling vanloads of it into Galway City, and Irish people smuggle Barry's teabags and coleslaw and brown bread onto the Costa del Sol every year so they can feel like they're at home when they're on holidays. Irish people pushed the boundaries of 'duty free' back in the '80s. There wasn't a friend going on holiday who wouldn't be asked to bring back a few hundred cigarettes. There were suitcases full of Lucky Strike being flown back from Tenerife and distributed to the neighbours. These days it's car boots full of wine on the boat back from France. We definitely have *caimiléireacht* in our blood.

Idir an dá linn
In the meantime

[id-der on daw lin]

Idir an dá linn, rachaidh mé ag obair ar an tionscnamh sin.
In the meantime, I'll get to work on that project.

> *It's a must for the 'but you'll never guess what happened in the meantime' moments.*

This is one for the mammies and daddies when you're teaching your child how to make the Rice Krispie buns for their birthday party. You might say '*Idir an dá linn*, melt the chocolate'. I think of it as meaning 'the time between us' – it has the feeling of a bridge in a conversation, when you want to get to the crunch point. When you say it, you're ready for the next part of the story. It's a must for the 'but you'll never guess what happened in the meantime' moments – 'Well didn't she go off to America and get MARRIED, Eileen.'

'*Idir an dá linn*' is a lovely, casual phrase, and if you can sandwich this into your spoken Irish then you know you're on the pig's back with the language. It's probably a phrase for the everyday Irish-speakers out there, the teachers and the students studying it in college, because adding this to your stories *as Gaeilge* will bring you up to Mícheál Ó Muircheartaigh levels of fluency.

Thaitin sé thar cionn liom
I fucking loved it

[ha-hin shay har keen lum]

Chonaic mé an tsraith sin The Bear. *Thaitin sé thar cionn liom.*
I watched that series The Bear. I fucking loved it.

I feel that way about chips.

This is a phrase for when you're really, really into something. The 'fucking' is there for emphasis, because it's what we would say in English if we ate something or went somewhere that we liked: 'I really fucking enjoyed it.'

You might use it for a film you saw, a book you read, or that perfect weekend away with your friends. You spent two nights in a great city and you had a ball. *Thaitin Lisbon thar cionn liom.* I fucking loved Lisbon.

I feel that way about chips. Every Friday in our house means chips for dinner. I'm very serious about my chips – sometimes they're homemade, sometimes they're frozen, but they're always swimming in vinegar. I have to ask them to triple-bag my order in the chipper to contain the liquid. There's nothing I love more than it being five o'clock on a Friday, you have the heating on, and the weather is horrible outside but you couldn't give a shit because you're about to fire up the chip pan. You get two slices of Brennan's bread, plaster them with butter, and then you start layering on your chips. You douse them with sauce and more vinegar, you flatten it down, and that's it. A chip sandwich on a Friday evening. *Taitníonn sé thar cionn liom.*

An-tóir air
In big demand

[on tour air]

Bhí an cluiche díolta amach, bhí an-tóir ar na ticéid.
The match was sold out, the tickets were in high demand.

You haven't really experienced trying to get a ticket for something that's in big demand unless you've tried to get one for the All-Ireland hurling final between Kilkenny and Limerick.

One of the most in-demand things I've come across in this country is Garth Brooks tickets. Nearly half a million people saw him in Croke Park and most of them went twice. I think Monaghan was empty. There's no other place in the world where one lad with a Stetson can fly in on a private jet, take millions of euro out of the country, and fly out again. I can imagine him out in his ranch in the middle of nowhere in America and his friends asking him, 'What are you up to for the weekend, Garth?' 'Well, I'm flying to Ireland. I'm going to play to eighty thousand people per night, and by the time I'm back here on Monday I'll have cleared about eight million euro. How about that for a long weekend?'

The only thing in more demand is All-Ireland final tickets. The media was in a frenzy about the price of the Super Bowl tickets when the Kansas City Chiefs played the San Francisco 49ers. They cost about five grand, but it was still the hottest ticket in town because every celebrity was there, from Taylor Swift to Brad Pitt. But you haven't really experienced trying to get a ticket for something that's *an-tóir air* unless you've tried to get one for the All-Ireland hurling final between Kilkenny and Limerick. Everything else pales into insignificance. They're like gold dust.

An dream sin
That crowd

[on dram shin]

Bhí protest *sa gcathar ar maidin, bhí an dream sin ann arís.*
There was a protest in the city this morning, that crowd was there again.

That group of people who just wreck your head.

'*An dream sin*' is for that group of people who just wreck your head. It's not about describing a lot of people, it's about a particular set of people. You can feel that there's contention and drama in this phrase. You use it for groups you don't agree with or groups who are annoying. We love giving out about 'that crowd' when we're watching telly or in the pub; I don't know what we'd talk about if someone wasn't annoying us.

Whatever your political views are, whether it's Féins, Fáils, Gaels, or Greens, there's always someone you'll disagree with, so '*an dream sin*' is a useful phrase to have at the ready. And it might just be a local crowd, the county council cutting down trees again or *an dream sin* in number 43 leaving their bins out all week and blocking the path. Even in English, 'the crowd' is wildly different to saying 'that crowd' – if someone uses 'that', you know they're about to go off on a rant.

Ag breathnú i mo dhiaidh
Looking out for me

[egg brah-noo ih muh yee-ah]

Tá tú ceart go leor, tá mé ag breathnú i do dhiaidh.
You're alright, I'll be right behind you.

An older brother or sister minding the 12-year-old on their first day in secondary school.

What a wonderful thing to know that someone is looking out for you. To have a mentor who gave you a start in your job and keeps an eye out for you, or an older brother or sister minding the 12-year-old on their first day in secondary school, or the coach on the local football team who will go the extra mile for their players – it's a beautiful thing. It's like having your own personal safety net, a person hovering in the background ready to catch you. Depending on where you are in life, you might be the looker or the lookee; either way, it shows a bond between two people.

'*Ag breathnú i mo dhiaidh*' literally means 'looking at the back of me'. It's the Irish equivalent of the English to 'have your back'. Everyone should have someone looking out for them. We won't always need them, but to know they're there is enough.

Ag dul amú
Going astray

[egg dull a-moo]

Chuaigh mé amú an tseachtain seo caite ag tiomáint i Maigh Eo.
I went astray last week driving in Mayo.

> *You might think you're lost, but you're not really: it's just an unexpected adventure.*

The word *'amú'* has been a cornerstone of my career. When I started filming the travel show, the series was called *'Amú i Meiriceá'*, which means to go astray in America. And *'amú'* was right because I was always up for divilment. I would be going mad on the streets of America or Asia, pushing the boat out to make the show engaging. I was just a lad from Navan conjuring up *craic* in Irish, and sometimes that meant dressing up as a ladyboy. Now, over twenty years later, the show has matured, so we've dropped the *'amú'*, but in a sense I'm still going missing – it's just that the places are more remote. But I'm still always up for a bit of *craic*.

'Ag dul amú' means going AWOL – you've disappeared. You can use it when you take a wrong turn in the middle of the countryside and you're four miles down the road before you realise your mistake. I've gone *amú* all over the world, but I still think there's nothing like going *amú* in Ireland, whether it's rural Tipperary or Dublin City. Because you might think you're lost, but you're not really: it's just an unexpected adventure.

Ainmneacha bannaí as Gaeilge
Band names in Irish

[an-im-na-kha baw-nee oss gwayl-ga]

Cé hé an banna ceoil is fearr leat?
Is breá liom Banríonacha na hAoise Cloiche.
Who's your favourite band?
I adore Queens of the Stone Age.

There I was translating Bob Marley songs and teaching them to a load of 12-year-olds.

By the time I was 16 or 17, I was a 'high prefect' or an *'ardchúntóir'* in St Mel's in Longford, and I would have to stand up in front of a hundred-plus kids between the ages of 11 and 13 and entertain them in Irish. We'd learn a dance for the *céilí*, we'd do some drama improvisations and I'd teach them a cool song for the *scoraíochtaí*, which were talent contests. This is where I came into my own; it was me, in charge of it all, and we were all having the *craic*.

Back then I had a load of badges on my jacket because I was mad into music. It didn't matter which genre:

The Police – *Na Gardaí*
The Doors – *Na Doirse*
Simple Minds – *Intinní Simplí*
U2 – *Tusa Freisin*

I tried to bring that love of music into my Irish, so there I was translating Bob Marley songs and teaching them to a load of 12-year-olds: *'Buffalo saighdiúir, i lár Mheiriceá.'* If I was still teaching there today, I'd probably have a few of these on the agenda:

Arctic Monkeys – *Moncaithe ón Artach*
Queens of the Stone Age – *Banríonacha na hAoise Cloiche*
Florence and the Machine – *Florence agus an Meaisín*
Fred Again – *Fred Arís*
Dave – *Daithí*
The Killers – *Na Dúnmharfóirí*

Braon
A drop

[brain]

Tá poitín álainn agam anseo, ar mhaith leat braoinín?
I've a lovely bottle of *poitín*, will you have a drop?

That single drop out of the tap after you turn it off, or you telling your friend that you'll have some whiskey but only a drop.

F*uisce. Uisce. Báistí.* Whether it's whiskey, water, or rain, if it's one drop, it's a *braon*. It is that single drop out of the tap after you turn it off, or you telling your friend that you'll have some whiskey but only a drop.

   I love to check the level of rain outside by peeking out the window at the car in front of the house. You can always tell by the volume of rain on the windscreen whether you should risk going out or not. If there's a waterfall coming off it, you're staying in; if it's a smattering, you might risk it; but if it's *braoinín báistí*, a drop of rain, you're fine. It's so light you're not going to get wet. Don't bring your jacket.

Chuir muid fúinn ann ó shin
We have been here ever since

[kur mwij foo-in aun oh hin]

Tháinig muid go Conamara in 1975 agus chuir muid fúinn ann ó shin.
We arrived in Connemara in 1975 and we have been here ever since.

A phrase for our travel genes, for the planned emigration and accidental relocation you hear about from time to time.

This phrase literally translates as 'We have placed our feet underneath us since that moment,' which doesn't really roll off the tongue, but it has an Irish charm to it. I saw it in a documentary on TG4 in 2023 about a photographer who had returned to Inis Meáin 50 years after first being there. They interviewed another Inis Meáin resident, the knitwear entrepreneur Tarlach de Blácam, who moved to the island from the mainland. At the end of the interview he said, '*Chuir muid fúinn ann ó shin.*' I love the phrase in English, so it was great to learn it in Irish.

It is a phrase for our travel genes, for the planned emigration and accidental relocation you hear about from time to time. 'How in the name of God did you end up in Finland?' 'Well, I came out here for a work trip, but then I met a girl and we got engaged, so I've been here ever since.'

Afterword: Irish is a superpower – use it every day

A few years ago, I sat in a small rural Hindu temple, maybe 50 kilometres outside Kuala Lumpur, with the local Tamil priest. He was a warm, friendly, well-educated man in his early forties, and his faith and devotion shone from his smiling face. I asked him to break down Hinduism for me. He told me that in Hinduism, life is about your teachers. Your first teachers, your parents, are the most important teachers because they are there at the beginning. After that, anybody who gives you a skill or teaches you something new is vitally important on your journey through life. Mams and dads are the greatest teachers on this planet, and I think the thousands of parents who are sending their children to *naíonraí* and *gaelscoileanna* all over the country are making a great decision. But if I had the power to change one thing about Irish, it would be the way it's used and taught in schools.

The current format of Irish as a subject in secondary schools isn't very attractive to students. I'd go as far as to say it's boring. It's not up to speed with a modern, changing Ireland, and it's certainly not cool. There is nothing new and fresh that brings energy to it. I would love to see more focus on spoken Irish, for learning the language as a form of communication to be more of a priority. The aim would be that all students would be able to converse in decent spoken Irish after 13 years of schooling, that it is a language to be used, not just to be studied.

I have total respect for the people getting their masters and PhDs in Irish, and I have so much admiration for the national school and secondary school teachers of our language. We have the best, most inspired, most motivated teachers in this country, and they should be the most well-equipped, well-resourced, and well-funded to do their jobs. If the teacher is buzzing and into the language, the students will be too.

I'm not a teacher, but I love sharing my passion for Irish with others. I'm just an ambassador for the language, and I'm lucky that I have a platform to share my love of it. But we should all look at ourselves as ambassadors for the language, no matter what level of Irish you have. It's there to be shared, in our kitchens, boardrooms, dressing rooms, coffee shops and pubs, at home and abroad. And it should especially be shared with the next generation. Because I believe anyone who speaks Irish has a superpower – and that power is connection.

Irish is a living language. It's for anyone and everyone. It has always been here, and it always will be here, as long as we keep sharing it, speaking it, and letting it evolve.

Go Raibh Míle Maith Agaibh

- Mícheál Ó Meallaigh
- Brian 'Bindy' Ó Broin
- Tí Chóil Neaine Pháidín
- Mary Ball
- Mícheál Ó Súilleabháin
- Linda Ní Ghríofa
- Matt Ó Brádaigh
- Scoil Mhuire an Uaimh
- St Pats an Uaimh
- Tí Maggie Tim
- Edel Ní Churraoin
- Tí Bhríd Johnny
- TG4
- Máire Ní Chonláin
- Fiona Ní Chléirigh
- Mairéad Ní Fhátharta
- Catherine Gough
- Evan Chamberlain
- Dympna, Rían + Shane
- Rosco O'Callaghan
- Liam Ó Maoladha
- Michael D. Higgins